BLESSED BEYOND
MEASURE

BLESSED BEYOND MEASURE

EXPERIENCE THE EXTRAORDINARY GOODNESS OF GOD

Gloria Copeland

New York   Boston   Nashville

First published by Harrison House, Inc. in 2004.

This FaithWords edition is published by arrangement with Harrison House, Inc., Tulsa, Oklahoma.

FaithWords
Hachette Book Group USA
237 Park Avenue
New York, NY 10017

Visit our Web site at www.faithwords.com.

Printed in the United States of America

First FaithWords Edition: September 2008
10 9 8 7 6 5 4 3 2 1

FaithWords is a division of Hachette Book Group USA, Inc.
The FaithWords name and logo are trademarks of Hachette Book Group USA, Inc.

Library of Congress Cataloging-in-Publication Data

Copeland, Gloria.
Blessed beyond measure : experience the extraordinary goodness of God / Gloria Copeland.—1st FaithWords edition.
p. cm.
ISBN-13: 978-0-446-51127-8
ISBN-10: 0-446-51127-7
1. Christian life.   2. Faith development.   3. Theology, Practical.
4. Conduct of life.   I. Title.
BV4501.3.C669 2008
248.4—dc22
2007047215

Contents

Introduction

For a number of years the message of this book has been close to my heart. I have come to realize that many people have an incorrect concept of God, which hinders them from coming to Him and receiving what Jesus died to purchase for them. At one time, I was one of those people. I'm so glad I found out the truth! Now I want everyone else to know it too.

You see, God loves every person and He wants to do them good. The Bible pretty well sums it up when it says, *"For God so loved the world, that he gave his only begotten Son...."* The Bible also says *"God is love"* (I John 4:8). Because of this great love, each person who is willing can receive salvation, healing, deliverance, peace, blessings, and every other good thing God promised us in His Word. In fact, understanding and believing the goodness of God is the very foundation for our faith.

This may not sound at all like what you have heard about God all your life, but it is the truth. The Bible says truth is what will make you free.

You are about to discover the true nature of God and how much He wants to bless you. He has already made plans and provisions to do just that. How can this good news become reality in your life? Read on, and remember: God is not mad at you. He loves you. He is a good God. Understanding this will change your life!

As you begin this book, pray the prayer for yourself that Paul prayed for the Ephesians in Ephesians 3:16–21:

Dear Heavenly Father, I pray that You would grant me, according to the riches of Your glory, that I be strengthened with might by Your Spirit in my inner man that Christ—the Anointed One—may dwell in my heart by faith. That I being rooted and grounded in love, may be able to comprehend, understand and have in-depth, working knowledge with all saints what is the breadth, and length, and depth, and height of the most powerful thing that exists. Let me know the very love of You Yourself—the love with which You love Jesus—which passes all human knowledge. Give me the knowledge of this love, Father, that I might be filled with all the fullness of God, because 1 Corinthians 13 says that love "never fails"! Now unto You, Father—who are able to do exceeding abundantly above all that I ask or think, according to the power that is working in all of me right now—unto You be glory in me, and in the Church by Christ Jesus throughout all ages, world without end. Amen.

It is good to continually pray this for yourself and for those you love.

Gloria Copeland

CHAPTER I

Understanding God's Goodness— The Foundation of Faith

[What, what would have become of me] had I not believed
that I would see the Lord's goodness in the land of the living!

PSALM 27:13 AMP

A few years ago, the Spirit of the Lord spoke to my heart very clearly. He said, *Preach the goodness of God and fear not the reproach of men.*

The Goodness of God.

It sounded like a simple subject at the time. But as I began to search out what the Bible has to say about God's goodness, I found it was a theme that ran from Genesis to Revelation. The more I studied about it, the more I found. It has absolutely amazed me to see how much the Scriptures talk about the goodness of God.

Why do you suppose the Bible—from front to back, Old Testament and New—would so strongly emphasize the simple truth that God is good?

Because it is the foundation of our faith in Him.

The more we know God's goodness, the more we trust Him. The more we trust Him, the easier it is for us to put our lives into His hands. And only by placing our lives in His hands can we open the way for Him to save us, and bless us, and work through us, so that His wonderful will can be done on earth as it is done in heaven.

I saw this firsthand in Healing School. When I began teaching on the goodness of God in healing services, I saw more miracles and healings than before. As people understood God's goodness, they found it easy to trust Him. That trust enabled them to open their hearts to His healing power. When they saw from the Word that it was the "Father's good pleasure to give" them the kingdom (Luke 12:32) and that "no good thing will he withhold from them that walk uprightly" (Ps. 84:11), they realized God was for them and not against them. The truth dawned on their hearts that He was not holding out on them. He was not trying to keep healing away from them. Instead, because He loves to do good, He was endeavoring to help them. Seeing that, they were able to relax and by faith receive what they needed from Him.

My prayer is that as you read this book, the same thing will happen to you. The revelation of God's goodness will help you receive from Him whatever you need.

Perhaps you have not yet taken the first step of your journey of faith because you've never received Jesus Christ as your personal Lord and Savior. Maybe you've heard about Him, and you even believe the things you've heard are true. You believe He is the Son of God, that He lived a perfect life and died on the cross to pay the price for the sin of all mankind. You believe He rose again and lives today. You believe what He said in John 14:6, "I am the way, the truth, and the life: no man cometh unto the Father, but by me."

Perhaps you believe all those things, but you've never opened the door of your own heart to Him. You've never said, "Jesus, I receive You as my personal Savior and Lord. I give You my life today!"

If so, you're not alone. Many people (even good, churchgoing folks) are in that condition right now. They know *about* Jesus, but they do not have a living relationship with Him. Despite their church attendance and even the fact that they know what the Bible says, their sins are still intact. They have not put their trust in the One who can save them. When it came to making a personal commitment to Jesus, they did not know what to do or they shrank back from making the most important decision of their lives.

I can only think of one reason why someone would be hesitant to make Jesus their Lord—why they would be afraid to give their life to Him.

They don't know how good He is.

They are afraid that if they give themselves to Him, He might deprive them of the good things they want and need. Fear makes them draw back because they are not really sure God has their best interests at heart. They do not understand the simple fact that God is a good God.

If that is your situation, I believe the truths you are about to read will provide the missing element of trust. They will give you the courage and confidence you need to step out in faith and surrender your life to Him.

Whenever you are ready, the salvation prayer is in the back of this book, immediately following the main text. Make Jesus the Lord of your life by faith right now, and you can immediately begin a change in your life and circumstances. Why wait when the goodness of God is available today!

You Can Trust Him with Your Life

Perhaps you are in a different situation. Perhaps you have been a believer for many years. You have enjoyed the blessing of eternal salvation. You know you are headed for heaven, and you have already tasted the goodness of the Lord in some areas of your life.

Praise God for that! But wouldn't you like to go further in your walk with Him? Wouldn't you like to be more bold and daring in your faith?

Think of the times when you sensed the Lord calling you to do something new, to make a change in your life. Like Peter, you heard the voice of the Master calling you across the water of life to new levels in Him. You heard Him say, *Come!* You wanted to step out of your little comfort zone and walk on the water...but you didn't.

Fear stopped you. You saw the wind and the waves in the circumstances around you. You grew timid and shrank back.

If so, don't feel condemned. Instead, let the truths in this book begin to strengthen your faith. Let them inspire you to research the Word and find out more about the goodness of God. Feed your heart on that goodness until your confidence grows, and you know you can trust Him, not just with your eternal salvation, but with every aspect of your earthly life as well.

Until you settle the fact that God is good and you can trust Him with your life, your faith is never going to be great because you will always draw back in fear. You will always be thinking, *What if He doesn't come through for me? What if He is not listening to me? What if He asks me to do something that will harm me in some way?*

However, once your heart grasps the goodness of God, you

won't be plagued by those questions. You'll be confident in the fact that He will never hurt you. He will never abandon you or let you down. As long as you follow Him, He will always be there—loving you, helping you, and blessing you.

If He asks you to, you'll be bold enough to walk on the water because you know His goodness will support you and keep you afloat.

God Isn't Confused

Of course, traditional religion has made people think they couldn't depend on the goodness of God. Religion has taught that one day God might make you sick. The next day He might make you poor. Some preachers have even said that God gives you things like sickness and poverty to bless you.

But that is religious tradition and it is contrary to the written Word of God. God is not confused about good and evil. He knows the definition of a blessing and a curse, and His definition is the same as ours. (That's because we got ours from Him.)

In Deuteronomy 28, you can read the blessings and the curses as He described them to the nation of Israel. He sums up the blessings in verses 11–13 NKJV by saying:

> The Lord will grant you plenty of goods, in the fruit of your body, in the increase of your livestock, and in the produce of your ground, in the land of which the Lord swore to your fathers to give you. The Lord will open to you His good treasure, the heavens, to give the rain to your land in its season, and to bless all the work of your hand. You shall lend

to many nations, but you shall not borrow. And the Lord will make you the head and not the tail; you shall be above only, and not be beneath, if you heed the commandments of the Lord your God, which I command you today, and are careful to observe them.

Later in that chapter, the Lord names every sickness, every disease, and all kinds of lack and calls them a curse. He summarizes the evil of that curse by saying:

> Your life shall hang in doubt before you; you shall fear day and night, and have no assurance of life. In the morning you shall say, "Oh, that it were evening!" And at evening you shall say, "Oh, that it were morning!" because of the fear which terrifies your heart, and because of the sight which your eyes see.
>
> vv. 66, 67

Obviously, God has figured out what's good for us and what's not. He knows it's good when we have more than enough natural provision in our lives. He knows if we plant crops, it's good to reap big harvests. He knows if we have livestock, it's good for them to increase. He knows it's good for our children to be blessed and for us to be physically healthy and whole.

On the other hand, He knows it's evil for us be sick, poor, frightened, and oppressed. Actually, the Hebrew word *shalom* that the Lord uses so frequently to bless His people means to have wholeness in your life—spirit, soul, and body. It means you have nothing missing, nothing broken. God knows that is the way things ought to be, and that is the way He wants them to be—not just for a few of His people but for every one of them. As Psalm 145:9 says, "The Lord is good to *all*."

You would think everybody would be thrilled to hear that God is good, but the fact is, it often upsets religious people—especially preachers. That's why God told me not to fear the reproach of men when He instructed me to preach about His goodness. Historically, people who preached it were highly persecuted.

In the 1940s when Oral Roberts began to preach about God's goodness, even men in his denomination criticized him for it. Others said it was too good to be true. One preacher said to another about Oral Roberts, "It makes me mad when Oral Roberts says God is a good God." The other answered, "What do you want him to say, that God is a bad God?"

"No," the first preacher replied, "but people will get the wrong impression about God!"

That preacher was the one who had the wrong impression about God, not Oral Roberts!

Of course, the real reason those religious leaders were upset was because they had spent years developing sermons about how God uses sickness, poverty, and pain to teach us something. They had developed great messages about how God is the source of all our problems, that when we get sick, He gets glory. (That's crazy. We don't get glory when one of our children gets sick, and neither does God. The very idea insults and blasphemes His nature.)

When Oral Roberts started preaching about the goodness of God, it ruined those preachers' favorite sermons. They talked awful about him. No minister in our time has been slandered to the degree he has!

In one particular city, he was preaching a tent revival, and the pastor of the largest church in that area went on the radio and criticized him. He warned the people to stay away from Oral Roberts' meeting. They didn't, of course. On the contrary, the more they heard this pastor criticize Oral Roberts and his healing message, the more people came to the tent meeting hoping to be healed.

Eventually, the crowds grew to about 10,000. As it turned out, the people were not offended by the message that God was good and wanted to do good things for them. They thought that was a great idea and they believed it. As a result, many were saved, healed, and delivered.

The Key to the Courage of David

When I think of someone in the Bible who truly understood the goodness of God, one person that always comes to mind is David. God calls him a man after His own heart (1 Sam. 13:14; Acts 13:22). As a young shepherd tending his flock on the hills of Israel, David fellowshipped with God and came to know His nature. He knew He was a loving God. He knew that He was good, kind, and patient. David knew that God would take care of him, provide for him, and deliver him from danger.

From that revelation, David wrote Psalm 23. My, what insight it gives us into God's goodness! You may have quoted it religiously for years. You may have even thought it referred to the care God gives us in heaven. But this psalm reveals what God wants to do for us here on earth—in the "valley of the shadow of death." It tells us what God wants to do for us while we are here in this present life where we must deal with our enemy, the devil. Praise the Lord, he will not be able to follow us to heaven. When God sets a table before us in that wonderful place, the devil will not be there!

With those things in mind, read Psalm 23 AMP right now and let it speak to your heart in a fresh way about the kindness and loving care God wants to give you:

> The Lord is my Shepherd [to feed, guide, and shield me], I shall not lack. He makes me lie down in [fresh, tender] green pastures; He leads me beside the still and restful waters. He refreshes and restores my life (my self); He leads me in the paths of righteousness [uprightness and right standing with Him—not for my earning it, but] for His name's sake. Yes, though I walk through the [deep, sunless] valley of the shadow of death, I will fear or dread no evil, for You are with me; Your rod [to protect] and Your staff [to guide], they comfort me. You prepare a table before me in the presence of my enemies. You anoint my head with oil; my [brimming] cup runs over. Surely or only goodness, mercy, and unfailing love shall follow me all the days of my life, and through the length of my days the house of the Lord [and His presence] shall be my dwelling place.

The more deeply you understand the truth of those words, the more you will be able to trust God in every circumstance of life. Your confidence in Him will make you bold when others are timid.

That is what happened to David. The revelation of Psalm 23 filled him with confidence in God. It made him bold and daring in dangerous situations. When a lion came after the sheep of his flock, David didn't run away. He single-handedly caught that lion by the mane and killed it. When the bear came, David killed it too.

Later in his life, when everybody in Israel was afraid of the giant Goliath, David was the only one courageous enough to fight him. He said, "Hey, I killed the lion and the bear, and when I get finished with this giant, he'll be dead too!"

What was behind this great courage? David revealed that in 1 Samuel 17:37 when he said, "The Lord that delivered me out of the paw of the lion, and out of the paw of the bear, he will deliver me out of the hand of this Philistine."

David not only knew about the goodness of God, he had seen it work in his life. He had seen the victories God's goodness had gained for him, and just thinking of them made him bold.

You and I will be the same way. The more we understand the goodness of God and the more we see that goodness operating in our lives, the more victories we will have to remember. The more victories we remember, the harder it is for the devil to talk us into letting him run over us.

When the devil tries to convince us that he's going to defeat us this time, he won't be able to do it. We'll remember victory over the lion and the bear in our own lives and think, *You know, God got me this far. He will not let me down now!*

I have had that thought more times than I can remember in the past forty-plus years. My life was such a mess when I first learned about God's goodness. I have often wondered, *What would have become of me if I had not believed to see the goodness of the Lord in the land of the living?*

I might not even be alive right now. I certainly would not be enjoying the blessings I am enjoying today. Over the years, as Ken and I have continued to trust God with our lives, we have seen the evidence of His goodness continue to increase until it has totally overwhelmed us.

The more I have come to know the goodness of the Lord, the more I have come to believe that God wants all of us to give our lives to Him so He can lavishly, without reserve, pour His blessings upon us. He wants all of us to be so blessed that everywhere we look, we see the goodness of God. Every time we drive up to our homes we say, "Look what the Lord has done!" Every time we get in our car and turn the key we say, "Thank You, Lord, for this good car!"

God's desire is for us to feel so good when we get up in the morning that we cannot help but be grateful for a well body that functions faithfully and feels so good!

Every time we look at our children and see the peace they enjoy, we praise the Lord. God's desire is that every direction we turn, we experience His goodness!

Notice, I said, "we." Not just me. Not just my husband, Kenneth. God wants to bless you too—in every area of your life. He wants to bless you spiritually. He wants to bless you physically. He wants to bless you in your finances, in your relationships, and in your career. He wants to give you the desires of your heart.

I know that sounds too good to be true, but that's not surprising. If you think about it, Jesus Himself seemed too good to be true. The fact that God sent Him to pay the price for all our sins, the fact that He died so we could live by simple faith in Him, sounds too good to be true. But it's true nonetheless. And Romans 8:32 says, "He that spared not his own Son, but delivered him up for us all, how shall he not with him also freely give us all things?"

Where Will You Be Next Year?

If you're still somewhat skeptical, let me ask you a question. Where will you be this time next year if you don't start believing to see the goodness of the Lord in the land of the living?

You'll be right where you are now. Things will be no better in your life. In fact, they'll probably be worse because the devil will still be unhindered in his work to steal, kill, and destroy.

But if you'll find out what the Bible says about God's goodness and you'll dare to believe it, things will begin to change in a wonderful way. Your life will immediately begin to improve. A year from now, you'll not only see that goodness on the pages of your Bible, you'll see it around you every day of your life.

That's what I call *living!*

CHAPTER 2

Will the Real God Please Stand Up?

The Lord is gracious and full of compassion, slow to anger and abounding in mercy and loving-kindness. The Lord is good to all, and His tender mercies are over all His works.

PSALM 145:8, 9 AMP

Ever since the Garden of Eden, the devil has been devising schemes to separate people from God. And the one scheme that seems to have worked the best for him is causing them to doubt God's goodness. He has been using it ever since it succeeded with Adam and Eve.

I'm sure you know the story. God provided a perfect place for Adam and Eve to live. He had given them everything they needed to live perfectly blessed and prosperous lives. There was only one restriction. The Lord told them not to eat of the tree of the knowledge of good and evil, warning them that if they did, they would immediately die.

Do you remember what Satan told Eve when he tempted her to violate that one command? He said, "You shall not surely die, for God knows that in the day you eat of it your eyes will be opened, and you will be like God, knowing...good and evil" (Gen. 3:4, 5

AMP). In other words, the devil said, "Listen, Eve, God lied to you. He's not trying to protect you from harm. He's trying to deprive you of something wonderful. He has pulled the wool over your eyes. He's not as good as you think He is."

Eve fell for it, then Adam. By their sin the whole human race was sentenced to spiritual death. And the devil has been causing people to doubt the goodness of God ever since.

Religions—even those based on Christianity—have portrayed God in ways that are totally contrary to the truths revealed by the Bible. Religious art, for example, often pictures everybody sad. It shows the Virgin Mary sad, baby Jesus sad, all the apostles and angels sad.

Religious traditions taught by long-faced, angry preachers have represented God as mad at the whole human race and looking furiously for someone to punish. The impression they give people is that God is in a bad mood, and you had better be very careful around Him because you don't want to irritate Him any further. Along those same lines, someone even wrote a song that the radio stations played some years ago. The chorus threatened, "God's gonna get you for that!"

If you have been made wary of God by those kinds of religious traditions, it's important for you to know the Bible does not teach any of those things. It does not reveal a God who is out to "get us" nor do us harm in any way. (Let's face it, we've all already given God plenty of reason to "get" us. If He had wanted to get us, we would have all already been "gotten" by now!)

The fact is, the Bible does not portray God being in a bad mood. On the contrary, Psalm 145:8–9 says, "The Lord is gracious, and full of compassion; slow to anger, and of great mercy. The Lord is good to all: and his tender mercies are over all his works." The word *gracious* means "disposed to show favors." So that verse is telling us God is always in a favorable mood. You never catch Him having a bad day. It's a good thing too, because He is so powerful that if He had just one bad day, we would all be wiped out. God is love every day. His mercy endures forever!

Of course, it is not just Christian religious tradition that has depicted God as angry and vindictive. Heathen religions depict their gods that way too. The difference is, that is an accurate picture of their gods, because they are not gods at all—they are demonic spirits. People who worshiped demon gods throughout history often believed they had to hurt themselves or someone they loved, in some way, in order to appease their gods' anger. Heathen worship in Old Testament times required people to sacrifice their own children, burning them in fire on the altars of false gods. It was a terrible thing.

Other pagan gods were not so harsh, yet it seemed they all needed something, offerings of fruit or gifts of some kind, to make them happy. But our God is not like that! We don't have to do penance or make sacrifices to appease Him. He Himself has already provided the sacrifice for sin in the person of His Son. In fact, the Bible says that God

> through Jesus Christ reconciled us to Himself [received us into favor, brought us into harmony with Himself].... It was God [personally present] in Christ, reconciling and restoring the world to favor with Himself, not counting up

and holding against [men] their trespasses [but cancelling them], and committing to us the message of reconciliation (of the restoration to favor).

2 Corinthians 5:18, 19 AMP

The moment we receive Jesus as Savior and Lord, we find that God is already happy with us. We don't have to bring Him plates of fruit to make Him happy. He's already happy!

What He's doing now is looking for opportunities to do us good and show us favor. You know how people who have hobbies like fishing or golf are always looking for opportunities to do those things? You might say God's favorite pastime is doing good for someone.

Ecclesiastes 3:12–13 says, "For a man to rejoice, and to do good in his life. And also that every man should eat and drink, and enjoy the good of all his labour, it is the gift of God." God wants to give good gifts to people. It's what He loves and enjoys. He is Jehovah the Good.

Often when I think of how good-natured God is, I'm reminded of my grandfather. All of his grandchildren called him "Pop." Pop was a truly good, kindhearted man, and he loved to do good things for everyone, especially his grandchildren. We quickly figured out that he would say yes to almost anything we asked him to do. I never remember him saying no.

Even before I had my driver's license, he let me drive his pickup around the Arkansas countryside. I remember times he even let me take it to the movies in a nearby town.

If my grandmother had not been there to stop him, I think

Pop would have given us anything we wanted. Although it has been many years since he passed over, every time our family gets together we talk about Pop. It makes us happy just to remember how good he was to us.

Being in the presence of someone who likes to do good for you makes you happy, doesn't it? Sure it does! That's one reason the Bible says in the presence of God is fullness of joy (Ps. 16:11).

Those religious artists who painted all God's people looking sad were mistaken. God's people are not sad. Heaven is not sad. It's the most fun place you'll ever go. If you think gathering together with all the saints in heaven is going to be like somebody's funeral, you are going to be shocked. People shout, dance, laugh, and have a glorious time up there!

Sometimes it makes me laugh to think about the adjustment some traditionally religious people will have to make when they go to church in heaven. They will be expecting to sing a dull, dry version of Hymn 94 just like they sang every Sunday in their church service on earth. But there are not going to be any dull, dry songs in heaven.

I remember hearing about one person who had a vision of heaven describing the people there gathering for a big meeting. The choir came out dressed in their robes, looking very distinguished. Then Jesus walked in, and when He did, the choir got so happy they started kicking the backs out of their robes, dancing, and praising Him. There was nothing to hinder their experience of His love and His joy, so their exuberance overflowed! How could it be any other way?

It's fun to think about heaven in that light, isn't it? But we don't have to wait to get there to start thinking that way. We can start thinking about Jehovah the Good right now. We can start thinking of Him the way He really is—full of joy and full of love. Then we can have days of heaven right here on earth!

God in a Single Word

Actually, if you want to see most clearly what God is really like, all you have to do is study love because the Bible says, "God is love" (1 John 4:8). Many people equate God more with power than anything else. Though the Scripture clearly teaches that God has great power, I am not aware of a verse that says He is power, but it does say He *is* love.

These days the world's idea of love has been so cheapened and twisted that for us to understand the kind of love God personifies, we must again go to the Bible. First Corinthians 13 provides us with the description we need. It says:

Love endures long and is patient and kind; love never is envious nor boils over with jealousy, is not boastful or vainglorious, does not display itself haughtily. It is not conceited (arrogant and inflated with pride); it is not rude (unmannerly) and does not act unbecomingly. Love...does not insist on its own rights or its own way, for it is not self-seeking; it is not touchy or fretful or resentful; it takes no account of the evil done to it [it pays no attention to a suffered wrong]. It does not rejoice at injustice and unrighteousness, but rejoices when right and truth prevail. Love bears up under anything and everything that comes, is ever ready to believe the best of every person;

its hopes are fadeless under all circumstances, and it endures everything [without weakening]. Love never fails....

vv. 4–8 AMP

As you apply these verses to the character of God, initially you might be confused by the thought that God is not jealous or conceited, that He does not insist on His own rights or His own way. "Doesn't the Bible say that God is a jealous God?" you might ask. "Doesn't it say that He expects us to worship Him and do things His way by obeying His commands?"

Yes, it does. But notice here it says love does not do those things out of self-seeking. In other words, God isn't jealous over us for His own sake but for ours. He knows that if we worship other gods or disobey Him in other ways, we'll fall into trouble and get hurt. He knows the devil is out there waiting to do us harm and He wants to protect us. Everything God tells us to do is for our own good and protection. We're His children and He wants us to obey Him because He wants to see us blessed.

That should be easy for us to understand. We're the same way with our own children. For example, we don't tell them to stay out of the street just to prove we are boss. We don't make rules for them just to restrict them and make our own lives easier. We are trying to help them stay safe so they can live long on the earth and that things will go well with them (Eph. 6:1–4).

We love our children. It delights us to do good things for them. Most of us would like to prosper enough to give our child a new car when they get a driver's license or a new home when they get married and start to raise a family. But we can't do that if they can't be trusted to do the right thing.

If a child is rebellious and won't keep the rules of the road, you won't be able to give him a fast car because you know he could hurt himself with it. If he won't stay sober, you won't be able to let him have a car at all. You want that child to abide by the wisdom you give him, not because you're seeking your own good, but because you're seeking his good. You want him to obey you because that obedience will open the door for you to bless him.

According to Psalm 103:13 NASB, God is this way toward us: "Just as a father has compassion on his children, so the Lord has compassion on those who fear Him." He wants us as His born-again children to do well in life. He is not trying to keep us under His thumb by making us worship and obey Him. He is endeavoring to get us in the place where He can safely give us every good and perfect gift.

What's more, the Bible reveals that God's desire to bless us doesn't just equal but *surpasses* our desire to bless our children. Matthew 7:11 NKJV says, "If you then, being evil, know how to give good gifts to your children, how much more will your Father who is in heaven give good things to those who ask Him!"

God Won't Leave You Out

If you have been living a disobedient and rebellious life, right now you might be thinking, *Well, that's it for me. I've been doing things God didn't want me to do for years. I've disobeyed about every commandment I know. I guess I can't expect to receive anything from God.*

Yes, you can! And if you will look back at that passage in 1 Corinthians 13 again, you will see why. It says love is "not touchy or fretful or resentful; it takes no account of the evil done to it [it pays no attention to a suffered wrong]." God is always forgiving. The blood of Jesus washes away every sin, and no mercy is held back when you turn to God in Jesus' Name to repent of the wrong done.

"But I've failed so many times," you might say. "God has had to put up with more trouble from me than you can imagine. I'm sure He's given up on me by now."

No, He has not. I know He has not, because "love bears up under anything and everything that comes, is ever ready to believe the best of every person, its hopes are fadeless under all circumstances, and it endures everything [without weakening]. Love never fails." You and I might look at our lives and think there's no hope left for us. We might think we will never amount to anything. But God's hopes are fadeless where we are concerned. He sees what we can be in Him. Learn to lean heavily on 1 John 1:9: "If we confess our sins, he is faithful and just to forgive us our sins, and to cleanse us from all unrighteousness."

You might have walked so far away from God for so long that you think He has forgotten you. But He hasn't.

How do I know? Because Psalm 115:12 says, "The Lord hath been mindful of us."

He thinks about you. Isn't that a blessing? God knows right where you are at all times. You don't have to work to try to get His attention. He already has you on His mind. He is mindful of His covenant with you. He remembers those things He has promised you, and He knows exactly what it will take to fulfill those promises. He has already thought that through. Psalm 139:17–18 says God's thoughts toward us are plentiful and precious. "How precious also are thy thoughts unto me, O God! how great is the sum of them! If I should count them, they are more in number than the sand."

The New Testament bears that out, reminding us that "He [God] Himself has said, I will not in any way fail you nor give you up nor leave you without support. [I will] not, [I will] not, [I will] not in any degree leave you helpless nor forsake nor let [you] down (relax My hold on you)! [Assuredly not!]" (Heb. 13:5 AMP).

Granted, there are times when we ignore God or disobey Him, and because of that we are unable to receive the help we need from Him. At those times, it may look like He has forsaken us. But that's our fault, not His. He did not forsake us. We forsook Him! He did not leave us. We left Him.

Even then, however, if we'll turn back to God, we'll find Him right where we left Him—waiting and longing to do us good. As Psalm 145:14–18 says:

> The Lord upholdeth all that fall, and raiseth up all those that be bowed down. The eyes of all wait upon thee; and thou givest them their meat in due season. Thou openest thine hand, and satisfiest the desire of every living thing. The Lord is righteous in all his ways, and holy in all his works. The Lord is nigh unto all them that call upon him, to all that call upon him in truth.

There may be times when you have fallen into disobedience and feel so unworthy that you are tempted to think you are going to be left out of God's blessings. But don't believe that. Remember, the Scripture says if you will call on Him, He will raise you back up into fellowship with Him. Remember it says He is good to *all*. *All* means *every person in existence anywhere*. It guarantees that you will not be left out unless you want to be. God will not leave you out. His promises are given to everyone. If you will reach out to Him in Jesus' Name, you will receive from Him.

You Won't Be Disappointed

I also love the phrase in that passage that says, "Thou openest thine hand and satisfiest the desire of every living thing" (v. 16). God is so good, He always has an open hand to us. He is never tight-fisted. We may have wandered far away from God, but if we just call upon Him in truth, we find He is near. We find He is right there ready to give us whatever we need.

One of the most beautiful examples of this truth I have ever seen took place in the life of a young girl who attended Healing School some years ago. A car accident had left her paralyzed on one side of her body, and she wanted to turn to God for help. The problem was, she had been living in disobedience to Him. Right before Healing School started, she had even stolen some tapes from one of our tables!

Of course, she was feeling terrible about herself. Her heart was condemning her, and she didn't think God would do anything for someone as awful as she was. But during Healing School, I read James 5:15: "The prayer of faith shall save the sick, and the Lord shall raise him up; and if he have committed sins, they shall be forgiven him."

Thank God, that precious girl simply took God at His Word that day. She received His forgiveness, and God healed her then and there. She walked to the front of the meeting and gave her testimony of stealing, repenting, and being healed!

If you have been disobedient to God, you can do the same thing today. You can repent and say:

> Lord, I know I've sinned. I've done things I knew You didn't want me to do. I've been walking away from You instead of toward You. But I'm turning around today. I ask You to forgive me and cleanse me of all unrighteousness. By faith, I receive that cleansing through the blood of Jesus and right-standing with You in His Name. I set my heart to obey You for the rest of my life. With Your help I will do what You want me to do.

Before now you might have been afraid to make that commitment to God. You might have drawn back from the idea of doing whatever He asked you to do. But now you can make that promise boldly, knowing that whatever He tells you to do will always be for your good.

I can tell you not only from the Bible but from experience (my own and others'), you will never regret choosing to obey the Lord. I have never in my life met someone who steadfastly trusted and obeyed Him who regretted it. Quite the opposite is true. Every child of God who has known and trusted His goodness has been eternally glad he did. Each one could say for himself the words of Psalm 34:1–10 NKJV:

> I will bless the Lord at all times; His praise shall continually be in my mouth. My soul shall make its boast in the Lord; the humble shall hear of it and be glad. Oh, magnify the Lord with me, and let us exalt His name together.

I sought the Lord, and He heard me, and delivered me from all my fears. They looked to Him and were radiant, and their faces were not ashamed. This poor man cried out, and the Lord heard him, and saved him out of all his troubles. The angel of the Lord encamps all around those who fear Him, and delivers them. Oh, taste and see that the Lord is good; blessed is the man who trusts in Him! Oh, fear the Lord, you His saints! There is no want to those who fear Him. The young lions lack and suffer hunger; but those who seek the Lord shall not lack any good thing.

The moment you are tempted to draw back in fear from something God tells you to do, remember this: God is a good God. He will only lead you in paths that will ultimately bring you blessing and increase.

True, sometimes those paths are not easy. But you can rest assured, they will always take you to good places. In the end, you will find that the difficulties along the road were nothing compared to the reward.

CHAPTER 3

Tracking God's Goodness through the Bible

O give thanks unto the Lord; for he is good: because
his mercy endureth for ever. Let Israel now say, that his mercy
endureth for ever. Let the house of Aaron now say, that his mercy
endureth for ever. Let them now that fear the Lord say,
that his mercy endureth for ever.

PSALM 118:1–4

"I don't like to ask God for much...just enough for me and my family to get by."

Have you ever heard anyone say something like that? You probably have. You may have even said it yourself. If so, it's understandable.

Somehow, many people have developed the impression that God is stingy, and if He blesses us at all He will only do it in meager doses. They have accepted the idea that He is pleased when we have barely enough and He is annoyed when we ask for more.

Where do people get that impression?

They certainly don't get it from the Bible. In fact, the more I read and study the Bible, the more amazed I am that the devil has been able to successfully sell such lies about God. A minister I know once said, "The Bible is so simple, we need help to misunderstand it." We have had a lot of help, because from the Old Testament all the way through the New Testament, the Bible testifies of the generosity of God. Page after page speaks of His love, His goodness, and His desire to lavish upon His obedient people more blessings than they can even imagine without the revelation of Him.

In the Beginning

Actually, if you want to find out just how much God wants to bless us and how good He wants our lives to be, all you have to do is read Genesis 1. That's right. God reveals His desire, His perfect will for mankind, in the very first chapter of the Bible. There we can see God's original intent. We can see what things were like on earth when God's will was being done before sin and death came.

In the first verses of Genesis, we see what kind of home God was preparing the earth to be as a dwelling place for the man He was about to create. It tells us that He spoke and brought forth the light... *and it was good.* He separated the waters from the dry land... *and it was good.* He created every kind of tree and vegetation to bear fruit... *and it was good.* He made the sun and moon, the birds, the animals, and the fish... *and they were all good.*

Then God made Adam, gave him dominion, and said:

Behold, I have given you every herb bearing seed, which is upon the face of all the earth, and every tree, in the which is the fruit of a tree yielding seed; to you it shall be for meat. And to every beast of the earth, and to every fowl of the air, and to every thing that creepeth upon the earth, wherein there is life, I have given every green herb for meat: and it was so. And God saw every thing that he had made, and, behold, it was very good....

Genesis 1:29–31

Over and over again in the first chapter of the first book of the Bible, we see that God created everything *good*. He did not create it to be marginal. He did not create it to be just okay. When He finished, He inspected His work and was satisfied everything He made for His family was very good: "And God saw every thing that he had made, and, behold, it was very good" (Gen. 1:31).

In Genesis 2, we read that God planted a garden for Adam's home, and He called it Eden. Do you know what the word *Eden* means? It means "delight."[1] Remember, God did not plant this garden for Himself. He already had a good place to live. (Heaven is a very good place to live, don't you think? Heaven is the permanent address for God and His family.) God wanted to make this delightful place not for Himself but for His people to live in and enjoy. He made it a place where they had the best of everything in abundance, with nothing missing and nothing broken.

In the Garden of Eden, God put "every tree that is pleasant to the sight or to be desired—good (suitable, pleasant) for food" (Gen. 2:9 AMP). No sweating over a hot stove in this garden. The meals grew on trees. The weather was perfect. Everything was just

---

1. R. L. Harris, *Theological Wordbook of the Old Testament* (Chicago: Moody Press, 1980, 1999), p. 646.

right. There were no storms or catastrophes of any kind. In fact, verse 6 says it never even rained there. Instead, the land was watered by a mist that came up from the ground. Gold and precious stones were there (Gen. 2:12). It was a perfect place to live.

When God was finished creating the Garden of Eden, He saw only one thing that was not good—the fact that man was alone. Do you know what God did when He saw that?

I can tell you what He *did not* do. He didn't say, "Now, Adam, I don't want you whining about being alone. I've given you a lot of good things and that ought to be enough for you. I don't want you to think you should have everything you want, so I'll just help you get by without a wife."

No, God didn't say that, did He? That is not His nature! That is not His way! He wanted His man to have every good thing his heart desired. God wanted Adam to be so blessed that there would be nothing lacking in his life.

So what did He do? He fixed the one thing that was not good. He created Eve and gave her to Adam as his wife.

A Happy Life without Stress

Josephus, the Jewish historian, adds some further insight into God's intention for mankind in the Garden of Eden. According to his writings, Adam and Eve were in the Garden only a short time before they disobeyed God. God said to them:

> I had before determined about you both how you might lead a happy life without any affliction, care and vexation of

soul and that all things might contribute to your enjoyment and pleasure, and should grow up by My providence of their own accord and without your own labor and painstaking.[2]

Isn't that wonderful? God's original plan was for mankind to live a happy life without any affliction or pressure. God provided food on the trees. Nothing had to be prepared. You know it was perfect and delicious. They didn't have to cook anything. They didn't have to plant because the trees were already planted. He didn't want them to have to work and sweat in order to live, as they had to do after they sinned and were forced to leave the Garden. He didn't want them to have to struggle along, barely getting by and trying to survive on their own. He wanted them to live by His blessing. He wanted them to live by His providence.

I like that word *providence*. It means "the act of providing provision, preparation, timely care and active foresight accompanied with a procurement of what is necessary for future use." It also means "skill, wisdom or management." God made every provision and preparation necessary for Adam and Eve to live in perfect blessing. He used His skill and wisdom to plan out the course of their lives and to lead them into every good thing by His benevolent guidance.

But they threw it all away. By rebellion against God's directions, they shut themselves off from His glory and condemned the whole human race to be born into sin. "For all have sinned, and come short of the glory of God" (Rom. 3:23).

Yet in spite of it all, the heart of God never changed. He imme-

---

2. *Works of Josephus* (Grand Rapids: A P & A), p. 26.

diately set in motion the plan of redemption. He immediately began making a way for mankind to reconnect with His blessings. He never gave up on His plan for man.

All the way through the Old Testament, God did everything He could do to help His people. He endeavored to provide the best possible life for them in this earth under the present dispensation. He gave them laws and said, "If you will do what I say, I will bless you and the curse will not come on you. If you will keep My commandments, you will have plenty. You will be blessed coming in and going out. Your storehouses will be full." He made a way for the curse of sin upon their circumstances to be resisted through obeying His Word.

God's Laws for Our Good

Most people don't realize that God's intent in giving the Law was to help His people reconnect with the blessings of His goodness. When they read the Ten Commandments or the Levitical laws of the Hebrew covenant, they think God gave those laws to people because He is harsh and demanding. Nothing could be further from the truth!

God was faced with a dilemma. Through man's disobedience, the devil had gained license to operate in the earth. By drawing Adam and Eve into sin, he had deceived them into bowing their knees to him instead of to God. Then, by using the authority God had given them, the devil began to impose his will on the earth. Jesus tells us what the devil's will is. It is "to steal, and to kill and to destroy" (John 10:10).

All mankind had been brought under the curse of sin, and God wanted to provide them with a way out. He wanted to give them a way to step back under His protective wing so He could shelter and provide for them once again. God knew in advance what Adam and Eve would do. His answer to man's dilemma was to send Jesus to deal with sin and bring full, spiritual redemption to the world. But it would take thousands of years for that plan to unfold. God was not willing to wait that long to start blessing His people, so He made covenant with them, essentially saying, "If you will obey My ways, I will personally take care of all your needs."

God's covenant with Israel was truly an amazing thing. It provided spiritual ordinances such as, "Thou shalt have no other gods before me. Thou shalt not make unto thee any graven image... Thou shalt not bow down thyself to them, nor serve them" (Ex. 20:3–5). If obeyed, those directions would protect people from being dominated and hurt by demonic forces on the earth because of Adam's disobedience. Other commands, such as "Thou shalt not kill" or "Thou shalt not steal" or "Thou shalt not commit adultery," kept people from being hurt and dominated by each other. The Ten Commandments that are so debated in our courts today were given for man's preservation and protection. Without these basic laws, nations live in chaos. There really is no debate about that!

Levitical law also provided instructions that would enable them to live safely in the physical world that had been corrupted by sin. History reveals that the laws God gave the Jews about such things as hand washing, purification, and foods helped protect God's people from sicknesses and diseases that destroyed other nations.

It took men thousands of years to figure out the truths behind God's laws. People used to do surgery without washing their hands because they didn't know about germs. Yet God, through

His laws, taught His people how to live so that sickness and disease would be unable to overtake them.

For those times when God's people did fall prey to sickness of some sort, God provided laws and commands they could follow and gave them priests to make a way for them to receive their healing from Him.

Through it all, God spoke to them about the coming redemption that would be provided through the blood of the Messiah. He gave them the promise of the spiritual deliverance that was to come. He told them that one day there would be a Savior who would pay the price so they could receive a new heart, a heart free from the stain of sin.

God never changed. He always desired to do good for His people. He always provided opportunities for them to step into His blessings. He was and is always good.

Jehovah the Good

God's nature and glory is so full of goodness that when Moses cried out to God in Exodus 33:18 and said, "I beseech thee, show me thy glory," God answered him by saying:

> I will make all my goodness pass before thee, and I will proclaim the name of the Lord before thee; and will be gracious to whom I will be gracious, and will show mercy on whom I will show mercy.... And the Lord descended in the cloud, and stood with him there, and proclaimed the name of the Lord. And the Lord passed by before him, and proclaimed, The Lord, The Lord God, merciful and gracious,

longsuffering, and abundant in goodness and truth, keeping mercy for thousands, forgiving iniquity and transgression and sin, and that will by no means clear the guilty; visiting the iniquity of the fathers upon the children, and upon the children's children, unto the third and to the fourth generation.

Exodus 33:19; 34:5–7

According to this passage, when you see God, you see goodness. Jehovah, the Good! He said about Himself that He is merciful, gracious, longsuffering, abundant in goodness and truth. God's mercy is so enduring, you cannot wear Him out. (Dizzy Dean, the famous baseball player, said, "It ain't bragging if you can do it." God was just telling the truth about Himself!) Second Chronicles 5:13 says, "For he is good; for his mercy endureth for ever: that then the house was filled with a cloud, even the house of the Lord."

We can tell from our own experience and from the experiences we read about in the Bible that God will wait and wait for people to turn to Him. Even when they resist Him, He will continually send them prophets and give them words to tell them what to do. The prophet Jeremiah preached to the same group for forty years. He told them over and over, "If you don't turn your hearts back to God and obey Him, the Babylonians are going to conquer your nation and put you in captivity."

Through Jeremiah, God told the Jewish nation everything they needed to do to avoid that end. He told them how they could be blessed and free. He warned them. He gave them the best plan. He told them what to do and what not to do. They refused.

Jeremiah was told to proclaim God's Word in the gate of the Lord's house. You need to read the whole chapter because it so reveals the goodness of God, but here we will quote just a few verses:

For I spake not unto your fathers, nor commanded them in the day that I brought them out of the land of Egypt, concerning burnt offerings or sacrifices But this thing commanded I them, saying, Obey my voice, and I will be your God, and ye shall be my people: and walk ye in all the ways that I have commanded you, that it may be well unto you. But they hearkened not, nor inclined their ear, but walked in the counsels and in the imagination of their evil heart, and went backward, and not forward. Since the day that your fathers came forth out of the land of Egypt unto this day I have even sent unto you all my servants the prophets, daily rising up early and sending them: Yet they hearkened not unto me, nor inclined their ear, but hardened their neck: they did worse than their fathers. Therefore thou shalt speak all these words unto them; but they will not hearken to thee: thou shalt also call unto them; but they will not answer thee. But thou shalt say unto them, This is a nation that obeyeth not the voice of the Lord their God, nor receiveth correction: truth is perished, and is cut off from their mouth.

Jeremiah 7:22–28

So what did God do? Just what He said. He let them go into captivity. What else could He do? He surely could not lie. God is not a man that He should lie.

Numbers 23:19 in *The Amplified Bible* says, "God is not a man, that He should tell or act a lie, neither the son of man, that He should feel repentance or compunction [for what He has promised]. Has He said and shall He not do it? Or has He spoken and shall He not make it good?"

He was not going to force them to do His will. He is never overbearing. He is never unjust. He is not a dictator. Because God is good, year after year He showed mercy and tried to get them to turn back to Him. They refused. Now, you tell me—what was God's will in the matter? That's right! His will was for them to obey so that He could do them good. Who determined their outcome? They did—by their own choice and actions. Their refusal to obey God put them into captivity.

Christians and sinners get confused about the sovereignty of God and blame calamities, accidents, tragedies, sickness, and the results of the curse on God. They think everything that happens has to be God's will because He is sovereign.

Yes, God is sovereign. Things are going to be just as He says, exactly as we saw in Jeremiah. He tells us the outcome of our obedience to Him and the outcome of disobedience. Then we choose our destiny and determine our end.

I call heaven and earth to record this day against you, that I have set before you life and death, blessing and cursing: therefore choose life, that both thou and thy seed may live: That thou mayest love the Lord thy God, and that thou mayest obey his voice, and that thou mayest cleave unto him: for he is thy life, and the length of thy days: that thou mayest dwell in the land which the Lord sware unto thy fathers, to Abraham, to Isaac, and to Jacob, to give them.

Deuteronomy 30:19, 20

This is the way God's sovereignly operates. He is God. He tells us what to do in order to make way for His goodness to be manifest in our lives. If we obey and walk in His ways, we will enjoy His blessing and live in "days of heaven upon the earth" (Deut. 11:21).

Deuteronomy 10:12–13 says:

And now, Israel, what doth the Lord thy God require of thee, but to fear the Lord thy God, to walk in all his ways, and to love him, and to serve the Lord thy God with all thy heart and with all thy soul, to keep the commandments of the Lord, and his statutes, which I command thee this day for thy good?

God is absolutely just and righteous. Remember that. *God is always right!* If things are not working, if things are not good—it's not His fault. He's not being hardhearted. He's not failing to listen or being unfaithful to you.

God has never withheld good from people who would obey Him. He has always desired to abundantly bless His people. That is why He gives us His Word—so we can receive it, do it, and be blessed.

But, we see in these passages, that His Word is a two-edged sword. We experience one edge if we obey it and the other edge if we don't. Evil is present in the world because of Adam's sin, and those who refuse God and His Son experience the curse of sin and death. God is the only protection from the curse. Obeying His Word is our only source of well-being. The good news is Romans 8:2: "For the law of the Spirit of life in Christ Jesus hath made me free from the law of sin and death."

God is so merciful. He will spare the disobedient as long as possible. He will give them every opportunity to change their course. If they do, He will forgive them and bring them back into His good will for them. If they do not, as Exodus 34:7 says, He "will by no means clear the guilty." He is no respecter of persons.

God Is Not the Problem

Actually, the book of Jeremiah will amaze you with the wonderful picture it gives of just how longsuffering God truly is. In Jeremiah's day, the Israelites were totally rebellious toward God. They spurned Him. They talked badly about Him. Though they gave Him no honor, He kept giving them time to repent. He sent them a prophet who went to them day and night, warning them and urging them to turn back to the Lord. That prophet, Jeremiah, said:

> The word of the Lord hath come unto me, and I have spoken unto you, rising early and speaking; but ye have not hearkened. And the Lord hath sent unto you all his servants the prophets, rising early and sending them; but ye have not hearkened, nor inclined your ear to hear. They said, Turn ye again now every one from his evil way, and from the evil of your doings, and dwell in the land that the Lord hath given unto you

and to your fathers for ever and ever: And go not after other gods to serve them, and to worship them, and provoke me not to anger with the works of your hands; and I will do you no hurt. Yet ye have not hearkened unto me, saith the Lord....

Jeremiah 25:3–7

Although Jeremiah was faithful, his patience was not as enduring as the Lord's and he grew tired of his job. He was fed up with the people because they wouldn't listen. They were always mad at him. He would tell them the word of the Lord, and they would put him in prison or try to kill him. He was not appreciated.

Some ministers today think they have it bad, but most of them haven't had to endure anything like Jeremiah did. Finally, Jeremiah said, "I'm not doing this anymore. I'm through!"

Now, you would think God would agree with Him. You would think God would say, "Okay, Jeremiah, it's been thirty-eight years now and these people haven't done one thing I've asked them to do. You can go somewhere else."

But God didn't say that. He was still reaching out to His people. He still wanted to give them an opportunity to change. He moved on Jeremiah, making His Word like a fire shut up in his bones so that he was compelled to keep preaching.

Even then, do you know what they did? The Bible says they turned their backs toward God and not their faces. They answered Jeremiah saying:

As for the word that thou hast spoken unto us in the name of the Lord, we will not hearken unto thee. But we will certainly do whatsoever thing goeth forth out of our own mouth, to burn incense unto the queen of heaven, and to pour out drink offerings unto her, as we have done....

Jeremiah 44:16, 17

God had promised them that they could possess their land, prosper, and have days of heaven on earth if they would just do what He said (Deut. 11:21). His will was for them to obey Him so they could be blessed. He had warned them that if they didn't turn from their wicked ways, the Babylonians would come, kill many of them, and take the rest into captivity. God did not want that to happen. That's why He warned them about it for forty years. Yet they said, "We don't want to obey You, God. We want to worship other gods. We want to be like the heathen and bake cakes to the queen of heaven." They made the wrong choice!

Finally, their time was up, and just as God said, the Babylonian army came against them. Still, God did not turn His back on them. He tried to help them even then.

In essence He said, "Okay, even though you rejected My first plan for you, I have a second plan. If you will give yourself over to the enemy and willingly submit to them, I will preserve you and I will bless you even in your captivity. But if you do not, you are going to die."

Of course, most of them did not do what the Lord said, so they died.

You might be thinking, *Well, that was in Jeremiah's day. What does that have to do with us?*

It has everything to do with us because the principles of God are still the same. If we want to live in peace, we need to do what God says.

When the Israelites went into captivity, they probably blamed God for it. They probably said, "God did this to us. He's the problem!" But God was not Israel's problem. He was Israel's answer. The problem was that when He told them what to do, they would not do it.

That's still the problem today. He tells people what to do and they won't do it. If we would obey Him, we could enjoy good days. We could have days of heaven on earth. Once we join in the family of God by trusting in Jesus, we don't ever have to have a bad day. If we have a bad day, we have missed something somewhere because God has made provision for us to enjoy His blessings. Most likely it's because we have not spent the time it takes with Him to hear what He has to say to us about our present situation.

A friend of mine says, "If you are a Christian and you aren't enjoying life, you aren't doing it right." That is absolutely scriptural. Jesus said, "I came that they may have and enjoy life, and have it in abundance (to the full, till it overflows)" (John 10:10 AMP). God wants us to enjoy this life!

God Refused to Quit

What amazes me most about the goodness God demonstrated to the Israelites in Jeremiah's time was this: Even when they blatantly said to Him once and for all, "We are not going to do what You tell us to do," God refused to give up on them. In His goodness and long-suffering, He would not quit.

As they went into captivity, God already had a plan in motion to gather them back to their land and bring them once again into the place of His promised blessing:

> For I know the plans I have for you, says the Lord. They are plans for good and not for evil, to give you a future and a hope. In those days when you pray, I will listen. You will find me when you seek me, if you look for me in earnest. Yes, says the Lord, I will be found by you, and I will end your slavery and restore your fortunes, and gather you out of the nations where I sent you and bring you back home again to your own land.
>
> Jeremiah 29:11–14 TLB

Think about all God had been through with those disobedient people! They had turned their backs on Him for forty years. They had rejected the God who loved them, the God who wanted only to do them good. Any human being would have washed their hands of a people like that. Any one of us would have just said, "Okay, go ahead and perish in captivity. You're just getting what you deserve."

Lamentations 3:21–23 says, "This I recall to my mind, therefore have I hope. It is of the Lord's mercies that we are not consumed, because his compassions fail not. They are new every morning: great is thy faithfulness."

God's mercies and compassions are new every morning. (They have to be so He can put up with all of us!) He still wanted good for His people. He still wanted them to be free. He still wanted to lavish His mercy upon them. So He looked forward to the future and said:

> I will make an everlasting covenant with them, that I will not turn away from them, to do them good; but I will put

my fear in their hearts, that they shall not depart from me. Yea, I will rejoice over them to do them good, and I will plant them in this land assuredly with my whole heart and with my whole soul. For thus saith the Lord; Like as I have brought all this great evil upon this people, so will I bring upon them all the good that I have promised them.

Jeremiah 32:40–42

Do you see how good God is? Even when His people have rebelled against Him again and again, He looks forward to the time when they return to Him. He gets joy when they do what He says so that He can freely come into their lives and do them good!

As Israel entered into captivity by their own choice and through their own fault, instead of condemning them for it, God gave them hope for their future. Just look at the words He said about their nation:

Behold, I will bring it health and cure, and I will cure them, and will reveal unto them the abundance of peace and truth. And I will cause the captivity of Judah and the captivity of Israel to return, and will build them, as at the first. And I will cleanse them from all their iniquity, whereby they have sinned against me; and I will pardon all their iniquities, whereby they have sinned, and whereby they have transgressed against me. And it shall be to me a name of joy, a praise and an honour before all the nations of the earth, which shall hear all the good that I do unto them: and they shall fear and tremble for all the goodness and for all the prosperity that I procure unto it.

Jeremiah 33:6–9

In spite of their disobedience, God said when they turned again, He would reveal to them the abundance of peace. One meaning of that word *peace* is everything that makes for man's highest good. Isn't that amazing? God did not tell them He would grudgingly forgive them and give them just barely enough to get by. He said He would give them an abundance of everything for their highest good.

Understanding God's Heart

Although God's merciful attitude toward the Israelites in the book of Jeremiah is amazing, it is not unusual. Read the entire Bible and you will find He was always this way with His people. Why? Because that's His heart. It's simply the way He is.

Over and over again, He would give them His Word. Over and over again, they would disobey it and suffer the painful consequences. Yet His heart always longed to do good for them. Repeatedly, He would say things like He did in Deuteronomy 5:29 NKJV: "Oh, that they had such a heart in them that they would fear Me and always keep all My commandments, that it might be well with them and with their children forever!"

God never looked at His people when they were in trouble and said, "I'm glad they're hurting. They're just getting what they deserve!" No, His heart longed for them just as our hearts long for our children when we see them being disobedient, getting into trouble, and suffering harm because of it. He longed for them to obey Him because He knew if they would, they could live free and victorious.

Repeatedly, He urged them to "walk in all the ways which the Lord your God hath commanded you, that ye may live, and that it may be well with you, and that ye may prolong your days in the land which ye shall possess" (v. 33).

What a great God! I said it before but I want to say it again: That is God's heart! He wanted them to live. He wanted things to be well with them. That's the reason He gave them His commands. He wanted to help them and do them good. In Isaiah 48:17–18, He said to them:

> I am the Lord thy God which teacheth thee to profit, which leadeth thee by the way that thou shouldest go. O that thou hadst hearkened to my commandments! then had thy peace been as a river, and thy righteousness as the waves of the sea.

That was God's heart in the Old Covenant, and He didn't change in the New Covenant. "For I am the Lord, I change not" (Mal. 3:6). You can hear it coming out through the words of Jesus as He sorrowed over the Jewish leaders' rejection of Him as the Messiah. He did not spurn them. He did not say, "You stubborn people! You've rejected Me and now you're going to get the punishment you deserve."

No, He said, "O Jerusalem, Jerusalem, thou that killest the prophets, and stonest them which are sent unto thee, how often would I have gathered thy children together, even as a hen gathereth her chickens under her wings, and ye would not!" (Matt. 23:37).

That's not just how God feels about the Jewish nation; it's how He feels about all people. He loves all of us with that same kind of tenderness and love. As John 3:16 says, "God so loved the world, that he gave his only begotten Son, that whosoever believeth in him should not perish, but have everlasting life."

He could say the same thing to each one of us that He said to Jerusalem. He could say, "How often would I have met your need and taken care of your children, how often would I have given you the desires of your heart—but you would not turn and listen to Me."

Because we didn't know God's heart and understand how good He is, there have been times in our lives when we've felt God didn't care about us. We had unmet needs, so we thought He had neglected us. But it was the other way around. We had neglected Him. He was always ready to heal our bodies. He was always ready to supply our needs. If we wanted something good, God was always ready to give it. We just were not in position to receive. God loves every person, but He is only obligated to the welfare of the person who receives Him into his life by believing and obeying His covenant.

Jesus, the Perfect Picture of God

As wonderful as the revelations of God's goodness in the Old Testament are, the best and most perfect revelation of it comes to us in the New Testament through His Son, Jesus. He is the fullest expression of the Father's heart. He is the fulfillment of the Hebrew covenant.

Jesus so embodies the character and nature of God that He said to His disciples, "Anyone who has seen Me has seen the Father" (John 14:9 AMP). Hebrews 1:3 AMP calls Him "the sole expression of the glory of God…the perfect imprint and very image of [God's] nature."

We know that everything Jesus said and did while He was on the earth was an expression of the will of God because He said, *"I do nothing of myself; but as my Father hath taught me, I speak these things….I do always those things that please him"* (John 8:28, 29). Therefore, if we want to know what God desires to do for us today, all we have to do is look at the ministry of Jesus and see what He did for people while He was on the earth.

Acts 10:38 sums up His ministry by saying, "God anointed Jesus of Nazareth with the Holy Ghost and with power: who went about doing good, and healing all that were oppressed of the devil; for God was with him."

In other words, Jesus went about doing good because *God is a good God.* According to this verse, we can know for sure that it seems good to God for all to be healed. Jesus said, "The Father that dwelleth in me, he doeth the works" (John 14:10). God the Father was involved in every healing and deliverance. We can also see the source of sickness. Satan is the oppressor. Read slowly and let what *The Amplified Bible* says soak into your mind and spirit:

> How God anointed and consecrated Jesus of Nazareth with the [Holy] Spirit and with strength and ability and power; how He went about doing good and, in particular, curing all who were harassed and oppressed by [the power of] the devil, for God was with Him.
>
> Acts 10:38

It is interesting to me that religious people in Jesus' day were no different from many religious people today. They were constantly upset with Jesus because He did not observe all their religious traditions. They got mad at Him because He healed people on the wrong day of the week. They criticized Him when He let His disciples pick grain to eat on the Sabbath because it violated their religious rules.

Jesus did not care as much about religious traditions as He

cared about *people,* because that's the way God is. When He saw people were physically hungry, He didn't just turn His back and say, "Well, they'll be okay. They ought to be fasting more anyway." No, He "called his disciples unto him, and said, I have compassion on the multitude, because they continue with me now three days, and have nothing to eat: and I will not send them away fasting, lest they faint in the way" (Matt. 15:32). Then He worked a miracle in order to feed them. It was the Father's will.

When people were spiritually hungry, He taught them.

When people were sick and they came to Him, He healed them. When they asked, He even went to them.

Religious tradition might say, "God doesn't always choose to heal you. Sometimes He will heal you and sometimes He won't." But the life of Jesus contradicts that statement. He healed every person who ever reached out to Him by believing and acting on what He said. Every one!

Just read the following accounts of His ministry and let that fact sink into your heart:

And Jesus went about all Galilee, teaching in their synagogues, and preaching the gospel of the kingdom, and healing all manner of sickness and all manner of disease among the people. And his fame went throughout all Syria: and they brought unto him all sick people that were taken with divers diseases and torments, and those which were possessed with devils, and those which were lunatic, and those that had the palsy; and he healed them.

Matthew 4:23, 24

When the even was come, they brought unto him many that were possessed with devils: and he cast out the spirits with his word, and healed all that were sick.

Matthew 8:16

Great multitudes followed him, and he healed them all....

Matthew 12:15

And whithersoever he entered, into villages, or cities, or country, they laid the sick in the streets, and besought him that they might touch if it were but the border of his garment: and as many as touched him were made whole.

Mark 6:56

And a great multitude of people out of all Judæa and Jerusalem, and from the sea coast of Tyre and Sidon...came to hear him, and to be healed of their diseases; and they that were vexed with unclean spirits: and they were healed. And the whole multitude sought to touch him: for there went virtue out of him, and healed them all.

Luke 6:17–19

Man-made religious tradition would have us believe that God is not willing to heal all who come to Him. It would have us think He demands near perfection from us before He is willing to give us anything. But Jesus proved that was not true.

Jesus demonstrated to us that God wants to meet the needs of all who come to Him in faith. Certainly among the multitudes who reached out to Him there were those who were just like people today—imperfect people who fail and make mistakes, people who by their own, natural merits do not deserve to receive anything from God. Yet Jesus healed them, every one.

At the wedding feast in Cana, Jesus showed us that when He was asked, He would step in to meet even seemingly insignificant needs. The hosts of the wedding had run out of wine, an embarrassing situation for them, to be sure, but hardly of great, eternal significance. Yet when Jesus' mother called on Him for help, He abundantly met the need by turning the water, not into ordinary wine, but into such wonderful wine that "the governor of the feast called the bridegroom, and saith unto him, Every man at the beginning doth set forth good wine; and when men have well drunk, then that which is worse: but thou hast kept the good wine until now" (John 2:9, 10).

That was so characteristic of Jesus! He never failed to give the best to those who came to Him in faith for help. He had such a good heart and He was so willing to help that He was an "easy touch."

"Yes," you may say, "that was how Jesus was back then. But does He still deal with us that way now?"

Hebrews 13:8 answers that question simply: "Jesus Christ the same yesterday, and today, and for ever."

Jesus is still an expression of the nature of God the Father, and the Bible says this about Him: "Every good gift and every perfect gift is from above, and comes down from the Father of lights, with whom there is no variation or shadow of turning" (James 1:17 NKJV).

Yesterday, today, and forever—God is a good God!

CHAPTER 4

Blessings Stored Up for You

But as it is written, Eye hath not seen, nor ear heard, neither
have entered into the heart of man, the things which God hath
prepared for them that love him.

1 CORINTHIANS 2:9

If this is the first time you've heard much about the goodness of God,
you may be concerned that I'm going too far. You may be thinking,
Wait a minute here. I know God is good, but there have to be limits
to that goodness. The evidence is all around us. After all, the earth
is full of people in need. It's full of people who aren't experiencing
the kind of goodness in their lives that you're describing.

That's absolutely true. Judging from a purely human perspec-
tive, there are, in effect, limits on the goodness of God. But the
limits are on our side—not on His. As we have already seen, we
limit our experience of God's goodness when we fail to listen to
and obey His voice as the Jewish people did in Jeremiah's day. We
also limit His goodness in our lives by our lack of understanding
and our lack of faith.

Think about it for a moment. Everything we receive from the
hand of God is received by faith and trust in Him. If a person is

bound by fear, constantly worrying about his own well-being and doubting God's care for him, he will not be able to reach out by faith and receive from His open hand. It is true that he may not be entirely at fault for his lack of faith because he may never have heard the Word about the goodness of God. He may be a sweet person who has been born again. But, even so, his lack of understanding will limit his ability to receive God's wonderful provision. It is his responsibility to seek God until he does understand.

One friend of mine tells of a time in her life that perfectly illustrates that fact. Born again at an early age and raised in a traditional, denominational church, she had little comprehension of the goodness and generosity of God. After she married and had children, she and her husband went through some financially hard times. Sometimes there just wasn't enough money to make ends meet.

Knowing they needed help from God, my friend would get on her knees and begin to pray, asking God to send them the money to meet her family's needs. Just as she would begin to ask, this negative thought would come to her: *How dare you ask God to meet your family's needs when there are children starving to death in China? You selfish person! You ought not to be praying for your own needs... you ought to be praying for theirs.*

Feeling ashamed, my friend would lay aside her request. "Oh Lord," she'd say, "forgive me for being so selfish. Just forget about my needs and send something to those poor children in China."

This cycle went on for some time until, one day, the Holy Spirit was able to get through to her. That day, as she began to pray, He opened the eyes of her heart. Suddenly, she saw a picture of her own head, and at the base of it she saw a little black dot. "What's that dot, Lord?" she asked.

That's the poverty mentality you developed from traditional teachings, He answered. *It's keeping you from trusting Me to meet your needs.* In the light of that revelation, my friend realized at once how foolish she had been. Why had she asked God to meet only the needs of the Chinese children and not her own? He is God! Certainly He has enough for everybody! Surely He could take care of the Chinese children and her family at the same time. Why couldn't she ask for both?

An Ocean Waiting to Be Poured Out

As you can see, my friend—good-hearted as she was—had been hindered in receiving God's provision for her family because of religious ideas she had learned since childhood. It was not because God could not or did not want to give it to her. It was her lack of understanding that kept her from reaching out to Him to receive by faith.

You and I may never have been tripped up by tradition in the same way she was, but I can assure you, everyone in one way or another stumbles over misunderstandings that keep us from receiving the full measure of God's blessing. The first step in removing those stumbling blocks is for us to understand that the limitations of God's goodness are on the human side. There are no limits on the divine side.

God is absolutely unlimited in His ability and His resources. And He is unlimited in His desire to pour out those resources upon us. We know of nothing that delights Him more than the opportunity to give blessings to His obedient children from His abundance. As Psalm 35:27 AMP says, God "takes pleasure in the prosperity of His servant."

One of my favorite descriptions of God's boundless capacity and desire to give comes from F. F. Bosworth's great book, *Christ the Healer*. It says:

[God] is always hunting for opportunities to gratify His benevolent heart, because *"He delighteth in mercy."*

Benevolence is the great attribute of God; therefore, if you want to please Him, move the obstacles out of the way of the exercise of His benevolence. He is infinitely good, and He exists forever in a state of entire consecration to pour forth blessings upon His creatures whenever they make it possible, which all may do. Imagine that the vast Pacific Ocean were elevated high above us. Then imagine it poured out and pressing into every crevice to find an outlet through which it might stream its flood tides over all the earth, and you have a picture of God's benevolent attitude toward us.[3]

Just imagine that! An ocean of God's goodness stored up just waiting to be poured out in our lives!

That is what the Bible teaches. Psalm 31:19 says, "Oh how great is thy goodness, which thou hast laid up for them that fear thee; which thou hast wrought for them that trust in thee before the sons of men!" A Hebrew translation of this verse says God has treasured up goodness for His "reverent ones."[4] He has abundant good

---

3. F. F. Bosworth, *Christ the Healer* (New Kensington, Pennsylvania: Whitaker House, 2000), p. 78.

4. Rabbis Nosson Scherman/Meir Zlotowitz, eds., *Tehillim/A New Translation With a Commentary Anthologized From Talmudic, Midrashic and Rabbinic Sources* Vol. 1 (Brooklyn: Mesorah Publications, Ltd., 1995), p. 377.

stored up for those who honor and reverence Him before others—for those who are not ashamed of Him and His goodness.

Remember the passage of Scripture we read earlier from Exodus where Moses asked God to show him His glory and God caused His goodness to pass before him? In the Hebrew Bible, the comments of the sages give us further insight into what happened there. It says that when God said to Moses, "I will make all My goodness pass before you" (Ex. 33:19 AMP), it actually means, "The time has come to show you as much of the divine goodness as you can comprehend."

Then it says God showed Moses all the treasures of reward stored up for the righteous. That's right! According to the Jewish sages, Moses also saw a large, unlabeled storehouse, and when he asked for whom it was stored, the Lord told him that it was reserved for those who did not have merits of their own.[5] It was a treasury of grace (undeserved favor) for those who didn't deserve it! That's how good God is. That's called *mercy!*

Yes, God has good things stored up, prepared, and ready for us. He has plenty on deposit to make every one of us wealthy beyond our highest dreams, free beyond our highest dreams, healed, whole, complete, with our families intact. It doesn't matter what kind of need you might have in your life, it is no challenge for God to fill it. He has much, much more than enough already laid up in store for you.

If that thought boggles your mind, don't worry about it. That's just the way God is. He is so good He's staggering. He is literally

---

5. Rabbi Nosson Scherman, *The Chumash,* 11th edition, Stone Edition, The Artscroll Series (Mesorah Publications, Ltd., 2001), p. 507.

more than we can grasp on our own, so He sent the Holy Spirit to reveal Himself to us. Throughout eternity we will still be comprehending Him. What a joy! Again, the account of Moses' encounter with Him bore that out when the Lord said:

> I will make all my goodness pass before thee, and I will proclaim the name of the Lord before thee; and will be gracious to whom I will be gracious, and will show mercy on whom I will show mercy. And he said, Thou canst not see my face: for there shall no man see me, and live. And the Lord said, Behold, there is a place by me, and thou shalt stand upon a rock: And it shall come to pass, while my glory passeth by, that I will put thee in a cleft of the rock, and will cover thee with my hand while I pass by: And I will take away mine hand, and thou shalt see my back parts: but my face shall not be seen.
>
> Exodus 33:19–23

In other words, God said, "Moses, you better stand back a little. What I'm about to show you is so good, so powerful, I'm going to have to hide some of it from you."

Insights from a Jewish Scholar

As we have seen in the story of Moses, the goodness of God and the glory of God are practically synonymous. In fact, the very word *glory* in Hebrew means "to be heavy with everything good." In our language, there are words that might be superior to the word *good,* such as *good...better...best.* In Hebrew, however, *good* is the superlative word. It speaks of the highest and greatest, everything that is positive and desirable.

The Jewish people understood that it was God's goodness that would deliver them. His goodness would bless them. His goodness would bring them victory. That is why, in battle, when they depended on the glory of God to go before them and defeat their enemies, they would proclaim, "For the Lord is good and His mercy endures forever!" (2 Chron. 20:21).

One Jewish scholar who had such understanding about the goodness of God was a man named David Baron. He was born in Russia in 1855 and brought up in a strict, devout Jewish family. His education was under the rigorous tutelage of the rabbinical training of the period. When he accepted Jesus as his Savior, he had wonderful insight into God. He wrote a number of commentaries about books of the Old Testament. In one such commentary on the book of Zechariah, he wrote some of the most powerful words I have ever read about the goodness of God. I've read them again and again, and they bless me each time. David Baron, quoting from another commentary of his day, wrote:

> "Goodness" is very frequently attributed to God in the Old Testament, as, for instance, in Ps. 31:19 [it says,] *"Oh how great is Thy goodness, which Thou hast laid up for them that fear Thee. Which Thou hast wrought for them that put their trust in Thee, before the sons of men...."*
>
> Goodness is that attribute of God whereby He loveth to communicate to all who can or will receive it, all good—yea, Himself, who is the fulness and universality of good, Creator of all good, not in one way, not in one kind of goodness

only, but absolutely, without beginning, without limit, without measure, save that whereby without measurement He possesseth and embraceth all excellence, all perfection, all blessedness, all good.

This good His goodness bestoweth on all and each, according to the capacity of each to receive it; nor is there any limit to His giving, save His creatures' capacity of receiving, which also is a good gift from Him.[6]

As I read David Baron's commentary, I was amazed. I thought, *How did this man get this revelation way back in the early 1900s? No one was preaching much about the goodness of God in every area of life at that time.* Then I realized he was brought up in a Jewish home. He was not exposed to the poverty syndrome and traditional teaching of God rewarding His people with oppression and lack circulating in the Christian churches at that time. He had read and studied the Old Testament scriptures and the writings of the Jewish rabbis who understood them. He saw clearly the scriptural truth about the goodness of God.

We Have a Better Covenant

God is good in the Old Testament...and God is good in the New Testament. He did not change in between. He is always the same God. He is always the same Father. The New Testament written after the Messiah came is just the next step in fulfilling God's plan

---

6. David Baron, *Commentary on Zechariah,* (Grand Rapids: Kregel Publications, 1989. Originally published 1918), pp. 332–333.

of redemption that is bringing mankind from the place of sin back to His perfect will where all good is fully received and enjoyed.

God did not provide more blessing and provision to those in the Old Covenant than He does for us. On the contrary, Hebrews 8:6 says we, who are born again of God, have "a better covenant, which was established upon better promises."

Our covenant is better because it includes all the promises of natural provision made by the old, plus the spiritual blessings of the new birth, freedom from sin and the baptism in the Holy Spirit that comes with the new—and all of it is ours right now! God has treasures already laid up for us just waiting for us to receive them, treasures beyond what we can imagine with our natural mind.

If you doubt it, read again 1 Corinthians 2. There you will find mirrored in the New Testament the promise we found in Psalm 31:19 that told of God's goodness being laid up for those who honor Him. In verses 7–10, the Apostle Paul writes:

> We speak the wisdom of God in a mystery, even the hidden wisdom, which God ordained before the world unto our glory: which none of the princes of this world knew: for had they known it, they would not have crucified the Lord of glory. But as it is written, Eye hath not seen, nor ear heard, neither have entered into the heart of man, the things which God hath prepared for them that love him. But God hath revealed them unto us by his Spirit: for the Spirit searcheth all things, yea, the deep things of God.

This says you and I will never be able to see with our natural eyes and hear with our natural ears the whole truth about the goodness of

God and His benefits. It has to enter our hearts through the wisdom of God that comes to us by His Spirit and His Word. This revelation of goodness cannot come to us from the outside. The Holy Spirit speaks it to our hearts, and then it comes into our minds and we begin to see the wonderful things God has laid up and keeps ready for us.

Think of it! Everything you need has already been prepared by God, and it is ready and waiting for all who qualify for this scriptural promise! Who qualifies? "Them that love him." Of course, loving God does not just mean going to church on Sundays. The Bible says to love God is to hear and obey His Word (John 14:21; 1 John 2:3–6).

The Amplified Bible sheds more light on verses 9–12 by translating it this way:

> What eye has not seen and ear has not heard and has not entered into the heart of man, [all that] God has prepared (made and keeps ready) for those who love Him [who hold Him in affectionate reverence, promptly obeying Him and gratefully recognizing the benefits He has bestowed]. Yet to us God has unveiled and revealed them by and through His Spirit, for the [Holy] Spirit searches diligently, exploring and examining everything, even sounding the profound and bottomless things of God [the divine counsels and things hidden and beyond man's scrutiny]. For what person perceives (knows and understands) what passes through a man's thoughts except the man's own spirit within him? Just so no one discerns (comes to know and comprehend) the thoughts of God except the Spirit of God. Now we have not

received the spirit [that belongs to] the world, but the [Holy] Spirit Who is from God, [given to us] that we might realize and comprehend and appreciate the gifts [of divine favor and blessing so freely and lavishly] bestowed on us by God.

God has blessings and benefits prepared and ready. The New Testament calls those benefits your "inheritance."

Somebody might say, "Yes, Gloria, I know I have an inheritance waiting for me in heaven when I die."

No, that's wrong. You don't get your inheritance because you die. You get it because Jesus died and was resurrected. He died to obtain this inheritance for you. It became yours the day you were born again. It belongs to you right now! God has made it and keeps it ready for you to receive whenever you call for it in faith. It is true that there are wonderful, heavenly rewards that are awaiting you after you pass over. But there is vast earthly blessing ready for you to receive now in this life.

Hebrews 1:14 calls us as New Covenant believers "heirs of salvation." Most people think salvation simply provides them entrance into heaven when they die. But if you'll look up the meaning of the word, you'll find it means much the same thing as the word *shalom* in the Old Testament.

The Hebrew word *shalom* is sometimes translated "peace" and sometimes translated "prosperity." In Hebrew it means "completeness, wholeness, peace, health, welfare, safety, soundness, tranquility, prosperity, perfectness, fullness, rest, harmony, absence of agitation or discord, to be complete, perfect and full." Now add to that the full definition of the Greek word *soteria*. It denotes "deliverance, preservation, material and temporal deliverance from danger and apprehension, pardon, protection, liberty, health, restoration, soundness and wholeness." Salvation includes everything in your life you could ever need—whether it is eternal security in heaven or a car to drive on earth. It includes healing for your body and a home for your family. It includes everything!

That's your inheritance! And it comes to you through faith in Jesus as the Lord of your life.

No wonder the angels said at His birth, "Peace on earth, good will toward men!" They understood that He was going to unlock the treasure house of God's goodness and make it available to all people everywhere. They knew that Jesus was going to obtain the whole package of salvation through His life, death, and resurrection.

They knew just how much that meant.

Living Memorials of God's Goodness

One thing is obvious, the more we understand and receive the goodness of God, the more wonderful our lives are going to be. Certainly, the Lord will take pleasure in that. But, according to the Bible, He gets another benefit from bestowing His goodness on us as well.

He turns us into witnesses to the world! We become walking demonstrations of the goodness and care of God.

The Lord has always wanted that for His people. All the way through the Scriptures, we see God wanting to give His people such abundance and such victory that it would get the attention of the heathen. He told the Israelites He wanted to bless them so extremely that "all people of the earth shall see that thou art called by the name of the Lord; and they shall be afraid of thee" (Deut. 28:10).

We have already read Jeremiah 33:9 where He said He would restore Israel with such goodness that "it shall be to me a name of joy, a praise and an honour before all the nations of the earth, which shall hear all the good that I do unto them: and they shall fear and tremble for all the goodness and for all the prosperity that I procure unto it."

Why does God want people to see and hear about His goodness in our lives? Because He loves them and He wants them to recognize Him as good and turn to Him! He wants people to know the truth about Him instead of a lie.

God wants to reach out to people through us.

I believe a lot of people are going to be saved in these days because God is showing them His goodness. He is giving them outstanding demonstrations of it. He is working signs and wonders that reveal to them just how loving He really is.

Sometimes people think of God as hard-hearted. They think He just expects people to believe what the Bible says about Him, and if they don't, tough luck. He won't have anything to do with them. But the fact is, if someone sincerely wants to believe in Him but they are struggling with doubts and misunderstandings that are holding them back, God is willing to help them by revealing Himself.

That is what He did for "doubting Thomas." The other disciples reported to him that Jesus had been raised from the dead. They told him they had seen Jesus and talked with Him. But Thomas couldn't bring himself to believe it. He said, "Except I shall see in his hands the print of the nails, and put my finger into the print of the nails, and thrust my hand into his side, I will not believe" (John 20:25).

How did Jesus respond? By showing him what he wanted to see. He appeared to Thomas and said, "Reach hither thy finger, and behold my hands; and reach hither thy hand, and thrust it into my side" (v. 27). Then he said, in essence, "Now, Thomas, stop being faithless and believe!"

As believers, we don't need to have signs and wonders to convince us God's Word is true. We already know and we are to stand fast in faith on what we know. But others, who have not yet been blessed with the revelation we have, are going to receive help from God. He will show them something to help them believe!

I am convinced He wants to use the outpouring of His goodness in our lives as one way to do it.

You may think that is a wild idea, but I have Scripture for it! Psalm 92:12–15 says:

> The righteous shall flourish like the palm tree: he shall grow like a cedar in Lebanon. Those that be planted in the house of the Lord shall flourish in the courts of our God. They shall still bring forth fruit in old age; they shall be fat and flourishing; to show that the Lord is upright....

According to that passage, one reason we need to prosper and be in victory is to show people around us that God is good. The word *show* means "to boldly stand out opposite, to manifest, announce always by the one present, to expose, explain, praise, certify, declare, expound fully, plainly profess, rehearse, report, show forth, speak." God wants His people to stand out boldly opposite so that others can see that there is a God in heaven. He wants to tell the world something through the lives of His people. He wants to tell them He's a good God!

The Amplified Bible says in verse 15 that God wants us so blessed that we are "living memorials to show that the Lord is upright and faithful to His promises." Think about the patriarchs, people like Abraham. Don't we get insight into the character of God when we look at their lives and see what He did for them, how He faithfully blessed them and kept His promises to them? Aren't they memorials that show He is upright? Yes!

Then it should not surprise us that God wants us to be so blessed that we are memorials too. He wants to be so free to bring the blessing upon us that we are blessed coming in and going out. He wants our lives overflowing with good. He wants people to look at us and see we are different. We are not worried. We are not depressed. We are prosperous when the economy is up and when it is down. Nothing seems to take us off our path. We just keep going on our way, blessed and full of the joy of the Lord.

Sadly enough, many times that is not the way it has been. God's people, either because of their disobedience or their lack of understanding, have not shown forth God's goodness. On the contrary, their lives were full of sadness and oppression, poverty and failure. The devil ran right over them. Their lives were like those of the Israelites described in Isaiah 52:5 AMP: "Now what have I here, says the Lord, seeing that My people have been taken away for nothing? Those who rule over them howl [with joy], says the Lord, and My name continually is blasphemed all day long."

When God's people are stepped on, put down, and defeated, God's Name is blasphemed. People speak ill of Him. They have no fear of God. When the world doesn't see the people of God with power and victory, they feel free to curse Him and take His Name in vain. They say, "Well, there's nothing to that God stuff. Look at those people who call on His Name. They have less good in their lives than we do."

Romans 2 describes a situation similar to the one in Isaiah 52. Rebuking those people who have called themselves God's children yet are living reprobate lives, it says, "The name of God is blasphemed among the Gentiles through you" (v. 24).

When the world sees the people of God talking one way in church and living another way, it causes them to blaspheme God. They think there is no power in Him. But when the people of God are walking in holiness, showing forth His power and His blessings, those who are living according to the world's ways become considerably more careful how they talk about Him.

One of the most powerful evangelistic tools we have is the manifestation of the goodness of God in our lives and the joy that goodness brings.

People are hungry for goodness. They are hungry for joy.

I believe it's time we showed it to them.

Don't you?

CHAPTER 5

A Good Plan and a Good Place

"For I know the plans I have for you," declares the Lord,
"plans to prosper you and not to harm you, plans to
give you hope and a future."
JEREMIAH 29:11 NIV

If I were to list all the good things in this life that God wants His children to have, this book would be as big as the Bible. The Bible says, "God...giveth us richly all things to enjoy"! (1 Tim. 6:17). I do, however, want to highlight two specific areas of God's goodness that I've found to be of special concern in the minds and hearts of many people. I want to address them very directly by telling you this:

God has a good place and a good plan for you.

I can almost hear some people thinking, *What does she mean "a good place"? Is she telling me God has a particular church or specific spiritual place for me to be?*

Although that's true, that is not what I am saying. God does have a church home for you. He has a place in His family that is tailor-made for your individual gifts and callings. But I am speaking about something much simpler and more natural than that. I am telling you I believe that God has a specific spot on this physical earth that He has prepared especially for you.

That may surprise you. Like many people, you may believe that God is so heavenly minded, He doesn't care about your natural surroundings. You may have thought He is too high and mighty to give consideration to something as small as the home where you live. He *is* high and mighty, but He also cares about every area in your life—natural as well as spiritual. I believe, in His providence, God has provided His every son and daughter a blessed and peaceful place that is theirs to inhabit and enjoy!

Read the Bible and you will see that land has always been important to God. He created it and it belongs to Him. Psalm 24:1 says, "The earth is the Lord's, and the fulness thereof...."

Even though He owns it, He does not need it for Himself. He created it for His family and He wants each member to have his part of it. That truth can be seen throughout the Bible.

As we have already seen, in the beginning He gave the Garden of Eden to Adam and Eve so they would have a place to enjoy their life and fellowship with Him in a peaceful habitation. He wanted a place where He could gather with them in the cool of the day and visit.

Every year our whole family spends a few days together in the countryside of Arkansas, where I was born. All our children and grandchildren come and we have wonderful times of fellowship there with each other and with the Lord. It is a great place where we can sit on the porch and talk together or ride the four-wheelers or go out in the boat. We appreciate it so much because it's a place where we can just have a good time together. And it's our special place! It is full of good memories and fun.

That's what God intended for the earth to be—a place where He and His family could enjoy each other. Just think what it would have been like for Adam and Eve if they had not sinned. God could have spent time with them just like we do with our family in the country. He could have gone out in the boat with them—and not just in the spirit! He could have talked with them face to face! He could have laughed in joy and delighted in them as we do with each other.

Of course, the entrance of sin into the earth created a different environment, but it did not change God's desire and heart. He wanted Adam and Eve to have a good place to live, and He wants us to have a good place to live. I believe He wants it to be a beautiful place too, because I see in Genesis 2:9 that in the Garden of Eden "made the Lord God to grow every tree that is pleasant to the sight, and good for food."

That tells me that God cares about beauty as well as practicality. God loves beauty. You can tell that just by looking at the earth. Even now, in its imperfect state, if you take a ride through the mountains, you will see breathtakingly beautiful sights. Consider what He created—rivers, lakes, sea, mountains, waterfalls, colorful canyons, lush forests, flowers—and you can understand how much God appreciates beauty.

I think God wants us to have surroundings that are beautiful and pleasant to us because that kind of environment encourages fellowship with Him. Think about it. When you go out into the woods or sit beside a lovely stream, if you know the Lord, it won't be two minutes before you begin to think about and talk to Him. Places like that are just conducive to communicating with Him.

God made Adam and Eve for a garden environment—a peaceable habitation.

A Garden Just for You

"Well, I don't know," you might say. "God made Adam and Eve leave the Garden of Eden. How do you know He still cares about our having a good place?" I know it because throughout the Bible, He continues to promise His people good places to live. Even today, places remain very important to God.

Look at Psalm 23: "The Lord is my shepherd; I shall not want. He maketh me to lie down in green pastures: he leadeth me beside the still waters.... Surely goodness and mercy shall follow me all the days of my life: and I will dwell in the house of the Lord for ever" (vv. 1, 2, 6).

One of the first things God talked to Abraham about was a place. In Genesis 12:1, He said to him, "Get thee out of thy country, and from thy kindred, and from thy father's house, unto a *land* that I will show thee."

When the Jews were taken captive and forced out of the land of Israel, the Lord promised to bring them back to that place and let them live there forever. He even promised them that when they returned "the wilderness and the solitary place shall be glad for them; and the desert shall rejoice, and blossom as the rose. It shall blossom abundantly..." (Isa. 35:1, 2). We are seeing that in our day. We have seen the Jewish people return to Israel and transform it from a barren wasteland into one of the most fertile, productive nations in the world. God has worked with them, blessed the work of their hands, and turned deserts into gardens in that land.

Even when God's people weren't living in the Promised Land of Israel, when they were in captivity in Babylon, He wanted to provide them with good places to live. He said to them, "Build ye houses, and dwell in them; and plant gardens, and eat the fruit of them" (Jer. 29:28).

Imagine that! Even in captivity, God wanted His people to have gardens. There is something about the natural beauty of gardens that blesses people's souls. God made us that way. That's why He did not put Adam on a freeway in a concrete jungle. He put him in a garden with rivers and trees. God likes putting His people in peaceful environments. In reading the Scriptures, I notice God talks to His people about gardens. In Jeremiah 31:12, He looks forward to the time when the souls of His people "shall be as a watered garden; and they shall not sorrow any more at all."

Genesis and Jeremiah aren't the only places in the Bible where God talks to His people about good places. There are many such scriptures. In Deuteronomy 8:12, for example, He promises His people they will build "goodly houses" and dwell in them. He also says He will give them "great and goodly cities, which thou build-est not, and houses full of all good things, which thou filledst not, and wells digged, which thou diggedst not, vineyards and olive trees, which thou plantedst not" (Deut. 6:10, 11).

Some of God's children like to build their own homes. Others would prefer to find one already built just like they want it. Either way you like it, God has a place for you!

Psalm 25:12–13 NKJV says, "Who is the man that fears the Lord? Him shall He teach in the way He chooses. He himself shall dwell in prosperity, and his descendants shall inherit the earth." One translation of that verse says that the man who fears the Lord shall "lodge in goodness." That's wonderful, isn't it—to live in a place that's a manifestation of the goodness of the Lord!

I can tell you from personal experience just how wonderful it is. From the beginning of my faith walk, I began believing for the right place to live. Since the reality of God's Word came into our lives, God has always given us a good home to live in. Our homes were not always big or fancy, but each one was a blessing to us. The first one was just a little house, but every time we moved, the Lord increased us.

Because I enjoy beautiful surroundings, through the years I cut out pictures and made notes of things I wanted in my dream home, which I believed we would someday build. I drew plans of my idea of the ideal house, changing them as I went along until, after many years, I had a clear idea of what I wanted. I can honestly say I was under no pressure even though the manifestation of it did not come for a long time. I still believed it would and I was in peace.

I prayed for about five years over whether to build or not because I knew time was short, and I did not want to waste time and effort building if Jesus were coming before I occupied it! I also prayed about the wisdom of God for this project. I prayed and listened for direction.

One day I went into a new home that was for sale. It was totally furnished and beautiful. I thought, *I could just move in here!* I got acquainted with the builder and began to work on plans. This took a couple of years while still praying about when to start and believing for the money to build and furnish it.

The plans were finished and it was time to act. Ken and I took some time off to pray and be sure this was the will of God for us at that time. (Timing is everything. The Bible says, "Prepare thy work without, and make it fit for thyself in the field; and afterwards build thine house" (Prov. 24:27). Psalm 127:1 says, "Except the Lord build the house, they labour in vain that build it. . . ." I did not want to go through all that effort in vain!) I enjoyed the home I had, and I would have been content to stay there, if that's what He had wanted me to do.

But the Lord let us know that it pleased Him to give it to us. So, we selected a site and began to build.

I don't mind telling you, that house is such a demonstration to me of God's goodness that almost every time I walk into it, I feel like shouting and dancing a little! It seems almost too good to be true. One day just as the construction was being finished, I walked around it and thought, *This is so wonderful, I feel like I'm in a dream.* Suddenly, I realized that was scriptural. Psalm 126 says:

When the Lord turned again the captivity of Zion, we were like them that dream. Then was our mouth filled with laughter, and our tongue with singing: then said they among the heathen, The Lord hath done great things for them. The Lord hath done great things for us; whereof we are glad.

vv. 1–3

God wanted the Israelites to walk in their dreams. He wants me to walk in my dreams, and He wants you to walk in yours.

Maybe your finances are in such a state right now that you don't think you will ever have a place that fulfills your dream. But I want to assure you, God does have a good place for you. The first place

He gives you might not be the place of your dreams. It may not be the place you ultimately live. Ken and I have walked with the Lord many years, and only in the last few years did we move into the place where we plan to live out the rest of our lives. Like us, you may graduate from one place to another while your faith continues to increase. But each one will be good and a blessing to you.

As you obey God and follow His plan for your life, "The Lord shall increase you more and more" (Ps. 115:14). Each day, as you learn to walk in the wisdom of God, not only your home and your place, but everything you need in life will come to you. As Proverbs 24:3–4 says, "Through wisdom is an house builded; and by understanding it is established: and by knowledge shall the chambers be filled with all precious and pleasant riches."

Just keep walking in the ways of the Lord, trusting His goodness, and He will lead you into a land of milk and honey. He will provide you a place where you can enjoy days as of heaven on earth (Deut. 11:21). He has a garden just for you.

Paths Prepared Beforehand

Notice, I said keep walking with the Lord and He will lead you. How will He lead you? He will lead you by the Holy Spirit, according to the plan He has laid out for your individual life. You know, God did not wake up one day when you were about twenty years old and say, "I guess I need to figure out something for this person to do now." He didn't just leave you on your own to come up with something to do with your life.

No, God knew you before the foundation of the world. Before you were ever born, He had a plan for you—a great, victorious, wonderful, abundantly prosperous plan. He has a calling and a purpose for every one of His children to fulfill. Some people think preachers are the only ones who are called of God. But the fact is, God has a plan, a place, and a responsibility for each one to do. He has callings for people in every walk of life. He has certain things for each one to do. He has created us in such a way that when we find His plan and begin to do those things we're created to do, we are happy and our lives are very, very good.

Ephesians 2:10 AMP confirms this:

> We are God's [own] handiwork (His workmanship), rec-reated in Christ Jesus, [born anew] that we may do those good works which God predestined (planned beforehand) for us [taking paths which He prepared ahead of time], that we should walk in them [living the good life which He pre-arranged and made ready for us to live].

Think about it. Living the good life! I can handle that. You are God's own handiwork. You are divinely designed to fulfill the good destiny God has planned for you. When you were born, God placed certain abilities, dreams, and desires within you that would help equip you for what He wanted you to do. Even before you gave your life to Him, while you were still a sinner, they were there.

Ken is a wonderful example of this. From the time he was a small child, he wanted to fly airplanes and be a singer. That was his dream. He did not want to go to college. He did not want to be a businessman. He wanted to fly and sing.

Of course, before he was born again he didn't use his talents and dreams exactly the way God intended. His singing at first, for example, was of the rock-and-roll variety. He sang it quite well, too. I wasn't there, but I've heard stories about how his singing caused the people to get out in the aisles and dance.

After he was born again and God called him to preach, the purpose behind his natural giftings became clear. The fact that he can fly airplanes has been a blessing to our ministry and enabled us to go around the world preaching the gospel in places that would have been more difficult for us to reach otherwise. His singing has also been a vital part of his ministry and a blessing to the Body of Christ.

So even before you knowingly begin to seek God, He already has a plan working for you. He has already given you some equipment that will help you walk out that plan. You may not recognize its true value before you give your life to Him because your understanding will be limited. Without His Word and His Spirit to enlighten you, you can never grasp the plan God has for you.

It makes me sad when I think about the millions of people who don't know what God has planned for them. If they only knew how good it is, they would rush to Him to get in on it. But because they never seek after God, they never know. They live and die and never discover the reason they were created.

That is why those of us who know the Lord want to share the gospel with every creature! We want everyone to have the opportunity to live out God's wonderful plan for them right here on earth and into eternity!

There are Christians who take the first step into God's plan by making Jesus the Lord of their lives, but that's as far as they go. They never read the Bible nor receive the Baptism in the Holy Spirit, so they don't experience the fullness of what God intended for their life. The purpose of this book is not to teach you about the Baptism in the Holy Spirit, so I'm not going to go into it here. (My book entitled *God's Will for You* will give you more understanding.)

But I do want to let you know that you will never see into the depths of the things God has planned for you and your life without the ministry of the Holy Spirit. He is our counselor, our guide, and our teacher. He is the One who leads us day by day. He is our helper and strengthener. You cannot go far in spiritual things without the Holy Spirit living inside. Ask Him in today!

Say, *Father, fill me with Your Holy Spirit. I receive Him in Jesus' Name.* Begin to pray and worship Him as the Holy Spirit gives you the utterance.

Beyond What You Can Ask or Think

Ephesians 3:20 says God "is able to do exceeding abundantly above all that we ask or think, according to the power that worketh in us," and I can personally testify that is the truth. When I was a 19-year-old girl, I did not have the slightest clue about what God wanted to do in my life. It was beyond anything I could ask or think.

My world was so small back then, I could hardly think beyond the little Arkansas town where I was raised. I didn't even have enough experience outside my own circles to recognize the fact that we were poor. We never went without food. We had clothes. And, according to what was around us, we were about average. There were those who lived in our community that I considered rich, but looking back, I see now they were not rich at all. They just had more than we did.

No one in my family was a turned-on Christian. My mother had given her life to Jesus as a young girl but I didn't know it. Spiritual things were a total mystery to me. I believed there was a God and Jesus was His Son. That's all I knew. I knew some things were right and some were wrong. I was raised among good people. The only thought I'd ever had about ministry was that I'd never marry a preacher, because the ones I knew I would not want to marry.

You may think I broke that promise to myself, since Ken is a preacher. But I didn't. Ken was not a preacher when I married him. He was a pilot. Of course, even then he was called to be a preacher, but that calling was very well camouflaged. I would have never guessed it was there.

Even after Ken and I answered God's call to the ministry and we were living in a tiny house in Tulsa while Ken attended Oral Roberts University, we had no idea how good God's plan for us was. I remember the day Ken went down to the riverbed to pray and God spoke to his heart, telling him that we were going to preach to nations. We received that word, but in the natural it was hard to imagine going to nations. We hardly had enough money to drive from Oklahoma to Texas to visit Ken's family. How were we ever going to travel to nations?

We did it by following the leading of the Lord, obeying His written Word, walking in His plan by faith one step at a time.

God Has a Plan and a Timetable for You

Those two words *by faith* are very important. You have to believe God has a plan for you or you will never be able to walk in it. You will constantly be worrying and wavering, and that will hinder you from hearing and obeying the Lord.

"But, Gloria," you might say, "how can I be sure God has a plan for me?"

You can be sure because the Bible says so in the Old Testament and in the New! Jeremiah 29:11 NIV says, "'I know the plans I have for you,' declares the Lord, 'plans to prosper you and not to harm you, plans to give you hope and a future.'"

Romans 8:28 AMP confirms this: "We are assured and know that [God being a partner in their labor] all things work together and are [fitting into a plan] for good to and for those who love God and are called according to [His] design and purpose."

Part of God's goodness is that He is a planner. And what a planner! He mapped out the plan of redemption before the foundation of the world so that when man sinned, that plan was in place. He had already designed a way to get us back into His will and reconcile all creation to Himself through Jesus. He already has the plan for the new heaven and new earth He will create one day. Everything He has planned for the earth will come to pass right on time. God never fails and He's never late.

If you study the Bible, you will find out that ever since Creation, God has worked on a timetable. He has had certain events scheduled. (They're called *moeds* in the Hebrew language.) Those events take place exactly at the appointed time.

When God promised to give Abraham and his descendants the Promised Land, He spoke about a time when those Israelite descendents would go into captivity in Egypt. He said, they "shall be a stranger in a land that is not theirs, and shall serve them; and they shall afflict them four hundred years; and also that nation, whom they shall serve, will I judge: and afterward shall they come out with great substance" (Gen. 15:13, 14). God kept that timetable to the very day.

Exodus 12:40–41 says, "Now the sojourning of the children of Israel, who dwelt in Egypt, was four hundred and thirty years. And it came to pass at the end of the four hundred and thirty years, even the selfsame day it came to pass, that all the hosts of the Lord went out from the land of Egypt."

When the Jewish nation went into captivity in Babylon during Jeremiah's day, God had already planned their deliverance. He told them that after seventy years, He would bring them back to their own land. After exactly seventy years, God raised up a heathen king who had a heart to rebuild God's temple and send the Jews back home. God's promise to them was fulfilled exactly when He said it would be.

Jesus was born at the appointed time. He was crucified and raised from the dead at the appointed time, and He is coming back at the appointed time. He won't be one day late. The Almighty God is always right on time!

In light of all these facts, consider this: The same good God who planned those events is the One who planned your life. His plan is for you to enjoy abundant life in Christ Jesus. He designed the plan, created you, and put in you everything you need to carry out that plan. When you were born again, he equipped you with the ability to hear His voice and obey Him in all things. He made you into a new creature who can walk in His power and wisdom. He has made you to be victorious. He filled you with Himself to give you power to fulfill His plan. He has wonderful plans, high hopes, and great faith for your future because He knows what you can do—with His help, of course!

It's Not Too Late

Right now you might be thinking, *Well, all that may be true but I haven't been listening to God and obeying Him. I've been doing my own thing for years and my life is so totally messed up, I don't think even God can fix it. I think I've missed my chance to walk out His plan.*

No, you haven't missed your chance. All you have to do is make a turn. I heard someone say the other day, "God allows U-turns." Instead of running away from Him, run to Him like you would run to a trusted loved one. Start going after Him with all your heart. God can take any life and any situation and turn it around. He loves to do that. He is just waiting for you to give Him the opportunity.

He will receive you the moment you repent and reach out to Him. He won't say, "Now, you just wait a minute, buddy. I think I'm going to watch you for a while and see if you are really sincere about this before I start blessing you."

No, God knows your heart. If it is earnestly turned toward Him, He will immediately start treating you like you have always been obedient and start pumping His goodness into your life.

Maybe you have even walked with God in the past and experienced some of His plan for your life, but you were drawn away from Him by some sinful bait the devil offered. You may feel like the country gospel singer who sang, "I got what I wanted but I lost what I had." If so, let me tell you, you are not the first to go astray. A lot of people have sold out their freedom and their life with God for something out there in the world. But even if you have done that, you can be like the prodigal son in the Bible. You can turn around and go home. When you do, God's mercy will be right there to greet you. He will say, "Welcome home, Son. Welcome home, Daughter." He will put a robe of righteousness on your back and bring you into that place He has prepared for you because He is good and His mercy endures forever!

What's more, no matter how much trouble and hell you've gotten yourself into, God has a plan to get you out. When anybody turns back to the Lord, He starts moving them back into the original plan He had for their lives. It's amazing what He can do.

One morning when we were overseas preaching, I woke up and heard these words in my heart: *God always has a plan!*

Isn't that wonderful? Even when to our natural mind things seem hopeless, with God there is always hope. With God we always have a good future ahead of us. Even when we have missed God like the Hebrews did in Jeremiah's day, if we will turn back to Him, He will say to us as He did to them:

> Then shall ye call upon me, and ye shall go and pray unto me, and I will hearken unto you. And ye shall seek me, and find me, when ye shall search for me with all your heart. And I will be found of you, saith the Lord: and I will turn away your captivity, and I will gather you from all the nations, and from all the places whither I have driven you, saith the Lord; and I will bring you again into the place whence I caused you to be carried away captive.
>
> Jeremiah 29:12–14

It may take some time for God to lead you completely out of the trouble you are in, and you will have to receive wisdom from Him to do it. But He assures us that "if any of you lack wisdom, let him ask of God, that giveth to all men liberally, and upbraideth not; and it shall be given him. But let him ask in faith, nothing wavering. For he that wavereth is like a wave of the sea driven with the wind and tossed" (James 1:5, 6).

When you come to God for His wisdom and help, He will never upbraid you. He will never condemn and criticize you. He will receive you and give you what you need to get back on the road to your divine destiny right then and there.

He'll start tugging on you by His Spirit, nudging you in the right direction. You might be flipping through the television channels, for instance, and suddenly you hear a certain person preaching and it draws you in. That's the leading of God's Spirit! That person might say something directly to you or quote a Bible verse, and you will find yourself wanting to open your Bible and look it up.

If you will stay sensitive and responsive to those leadings, you will find that God is always talking to you. He is always drawing you into His plan. That's why I believe you ought to get up first thing every morning and tune in to Him through prayer and Bible reading. He knows where you need to be. He knows what you need to do each day to stay on track. He knows the plan! Seek Him and you will see it too.

There may be times when you get to a plateau and you don't seem to be going anywhere. When that happens, it is never God's fault. He is always ready to help you. So when you get to a place like that, just dive into His Word in a greater measure and ask Him to show you where you've missed it. We all have to step back and regroup sometimes. We miss God's direction now and then. But when we do, if we repent, our loving heavenly Father is there to forgive us and help us get right back where we were and go on further than we have ever been.

As we continue obeying the promptings of His Spirit, God will draw us deeper and deeper into His plan. The same process goes on all the way through our Christian life. Even as spiritual adults, we still follow that inward witness as it leads us on the path of God's plan for us.

Sometimes you may find God calling you to do things you don't see how you have the resources to do. For example, I never thought I was able to preach. It was not even something I wanted to do. I was quiet. I did not like to talk in front of a crowd. But God maneuvered me until I knew that He wanted me to do it. And you know what? It's been the greatest joy and blessing of my life to be able to share the Word of God with others. It changed me for the better!

I don't care what you've been doing until now, if you haven't been in the plan of God, you haven't done anything yet. Nothing can compare with His plan for your life. You may have material riches but, even so, you will never experience true prosperity until you step into what God has planned.

I have found through experience that God's plan is so good that I don't want to miss any of it. I want to do everything He has called me to do. I want to run the race He has set before me. I know if I'll do that, not only will I hear Him say, "Well done," at the end of my journey, but I will also delight in His goodness every step of the way.

CHAPTER 6

Enjoying God's Best

*[The Father] has delivered and drawn us to Himself out of the
control and the dominion of darkness and has transferred us into
the kingdom of the Son of His love.*

COLOSSIANS 1:13 AMP

Whenever the subject of God's goodness is discussed among
people who are not students of the Bible, one question will invari-
ably arise. All of us have either asked this question ourselves or
heard it asked by others:

"If God is so good, why is there so much evil and pain in the
world?"

As deep and complicated as that question may sound, the
answer is actually quite simple. God is not the only one at work in
the earth. There is another spiritual being who constantly opposes
Him. Just as God is the source of everything good and perfect in
the earth and in our lives, the one who opposes Him is the source
of all evil.

If you've read the book of Genesis, you know the spiritual
being I'm referring to is Satan, Lucifer, or the devil himself—the
deceiver.

"If the devil is so bad," you might ask, "why did God give him authority to operate on the earth?"

He didn't.

Adam and Eve did.

Genesis 1:26 tells us when God created Adam and Eve He said, "Let us make man in our image, after our likeness: and let them have dominion...." God gave Adam and Eve—and through them, all mankind—authority over the whole earth. His intention was for them to use that authority in obedience to Him and govern the affairs of earth with His perfect goodness. If they had done so, God's will would have been done on the earth under His family's oversight and we truly would have had heaven on earth.

But as we well know, that is not what happened. Instead, they disobeyed God and submitted to the temptation of the devil. At the time, the devil was an outlaw in the earth. God had stripped him of his authority, because after he was created, evil was found in him due to rebellion and he was cast out of heaven (Ezek. 28:15, 16). He lost his first estate. Jesus said, "I saw Satan fall like lightning from heaven" (Luke 10:18 NIV). He was banished from heaven. When he approached Eve in the Garden of Eden, he had no authority to intervene at all in the affairs of earth or its inhabitants.

That is why he tempted Adam and Eve. He knew they had dominion and he wanted it. He also knew that if he could get them to bow their knee to him, he could use them and their God-given authority to exert his influence on the earth. Death came by sin, which came through their choice. By separating them from God and His life through sin, he could enslave them to his will and establish his own wicked kingdom through their authority.

That's exactly what he did.

To the devil it must have seemed like a master plan. But God, the true Master Planner, was way ahead of him. He knew what the devil was going to do before he did it. He knew Adam and Eve would make the wrong choice. And He had already designed a redemptive plan that would eventually deliver mankind from the bondage of sin and restore that lost dominion to all who made Jesus Christ their Lord.

God had already planned that, first through His Son, Jesus, and then through those who would become God's sons by believing in Him, the kingdom of God would once again come, and His will would be done in this world just like it is in heaven.

The New Testament tells us that one day the devil and all who serve him will be totally removed from the earth. In that day, things will be as God intended them to be in the beginning. Under the lordship of Jesus and those who serve Him, God's goodness will totally govern the affairs of this planet and there will once again be heaven on earth (Eph. 1:10; Rev. 11:15).

Until that time, however, there will continue to be two kingdoms operating here—the devil's kingdom and the kingdom of God (Matt. 12:24–30). Each one has a ruler as well as a set of spiritual laws and principles by which it operates. For us to live safely on this earth, we must be aware of them because we are always going to be under the influence of one kingdom or the other. There is no neutral ground. The kingdom of God has dominion over the kingdom of darkness. Light always overcomes darkness. Every person has been given a free will to choose where he lives and moves and has his being, and whose plan he follows.

The Kingdom of Darkness

Satan is the ruler of what the Bible calls the "dominion of darkness" (Col. 1:13 AMP). The Greek word translated *dominion* in *The Amplified Bible* and *power* in the *King James Version* can also be translated *authority*. Before His crucifixion, Jesus referred to Satan as the "prince of this world" (John 12:31). He is the ruler of this current, ungodly world system. The New Testament tells us that Jesus, through His death and resurrection, spoiled (or disarmed) the devil and triumphed over him and all his demonic hosts (Col. 2:15). So even though Satan's kingdom is still here, its operations can always be overcome by a believer in Jesus' Name.

For insight into the nature of the devil, all you have to do is take a quick look at some of the names the Bible gives him. They include such titles as *the father of lies* and *a murderer* (John 8:44); *the thief* who comes to steal, kill, and destroy (John 10:10); *the wicked one* (1 John 5:18); *that age-old serpent* who is *the seducer (or deceiver) of all humanity and the accuser of our brethren* (Rev. 12:9, 10 AMP).

The operating principle of the devil's kingdom is the principle of fear. According to the Bible, the devil uses fear to keep people in bondage (Heb. 2:15). Any time they try to break free of his control, he calls on the force of fear to keep them in line.

For example, if someone sees his employer doing something illegal and furthering a hurtful scheme of the devil, that person might very much want to interrupt that scheme by telling the authorities the truth. How does the devil stop him? By speaking thoughts to him that inspire fear such as, *If you blow the whistle on your employer, you'll lose your job. Nobody else will hire you*

*because you're a snitch. You'll go broke. You'll lose your house.
You'd better just look the other way like everybody else.*

Those thoughts have a familiar ring, don't they? Sure they do, because the devil sees to it that we have them. He uses those kinds of fearful thoughts to keep people under his control.

The governing spiritual law of the devil's kingdom is what the Bible calls "the law of sin and death" (Rom. 8:2). Every person under the devil's rule is doomed to a life of slavery to sin. And every person who has not made Jesus their Lord is under Satan's rule. When we come into the world, we are born into sin because of the sin of Adam. From Adam and Eve we inherit the sin nature.

The devil gives his people no choice. They may fight against sinful behavior in one area of their lives. But if they succeed in overcoming it, they will only find it cropping up in another area. Since "the wages of sin is death" (Rom. 6:23), death is continually at work in them, dragging them downward. Their lives go from bad to worse, eventually ending in eternal death and permanent separation from God. (And by the way, there is a heaven to gain and a hell to shun. At death you will be received into one or the other. Right now you have a reservation in one place or the other. The good news is, you can change it if you need to!)

Even those in the devil's kingdom who are able to obtain what we normally think of as "good things" in life are unable to maintain a lifestyle of freedom and joy. If they fall in love and get married, they ruin their relationship with things like selfishness or anger. If they get money, the money ruins them because money finances sin in their lives.

We see examples of that in the lives of unsaved athletes and entertainers all the time. In the Dallas area just a few years ago, for instance, a well-known football player killed himself with illegal drugs. He was a likeable person, from what people said. Everyone was shocked. No one was expecting him to do such a thing. But the fact is, if you have a lot of money, you had better have your head on straight because you can afford to do anything you want. You can buy all the drugs and immoral pleasures the world can offer. You will have to pay the wages—death. Sin cuts your physical life short. Death is sin's curb.

That is why so many highly successful entertainers die young. Money is a dangerous thing if you are without God and living in the kingdom of darkness.

The Old Testament describes the results brought about by the law of sin and death as *the curse*. Because Satan himself is cursed, everything he touches is cursed and everyone who remains in his kingdom is cursed. People sometimes talk about how the devil can bless his own. Actually, he can't bless anybody because he himself is cursed. Anything he could give to those under his rule will eventually destroy them.

One more thing about the kingdom of darkness: It has affected this natural, physical earth on which we live. Romans 8:21 says that creation, or nature itself, is right now in bondage to decay and corruption because of the curse of sin and death. Therefore, many of the natural disasters we see—such as earthquakes, famines, tornadoes, and floods—are not "acts of God" as they are so often called. On the contrary, they are malfunctions of a natural system that has been twisted by the effects of sin and the influence of the devil.

The Kingdom of God

The other kingdom operating in the earth is the kingdom of God, and it is the most powerful kingdom. Also referred to in the Scriptures as the *kingdom of heaven,* this kingdom is under the dominion of the Lord Jesus Christ. Although the Bible gives Him many wonderful titles, I think the one that gives us the greatest insight into His nature is the Prince of Peace. As we saw earlier, the Hebrew word for *peace* denotes wholeness, blessing, and prosperity. It means "to be complete and undamaged with nothing missing and nothing broken."

Just as the devil's kingdom is shaped by the character revealed in his names, the kingdom of God is characterized by the goodness revealed in the name of its king. It is a kingdom filled and governed with the peace and blessing of God. The moment we believe in our hearts and confess with our mouths that Jesus is our Lord and King, the Bible says we are translated out of the dominion of darkness and into that good kingdom—the kingdom of the light of God's Son: "[The Father] has delivered and drawn us to Himself out of the control and the dominion of darkness and has transferred us into the kingdom of the Son of His love" (Col. 1:13 AMP). At that moment, even though we still live on this physical earth surrounded in many ways by the devil's operations, our citizenship is transferred and we become citizens of heaven (Phil. 3:20 AMP; Heb. 12:22, 23 AMP). As citizens of the heavenly kingdom, we are released from the devil's operating principles and the laws of his kingdom, and we come instead under a completely new government ruled by a higher law.

What is this new law? The Bible calls it "the law of the Spirit of life in Christ Jesus," and this law frees us from the demonic law of sin and death: "For the law of the Spirit of life [which is] in Christ Jesus [the law of our new being] has freed me from the law of sin and of death" (Rom. 8:2 AMP).

Where Satan's law of sin and death brought us bondage and destruction, the law of the Spirit of life in Christ Jesus brings us freedom and restoration. Where the law of sin and death brought the curse, the law of the Spirit of life brings the blessing. The law of the Spirit of life will convey you from where you are to where you desire to be.

Not only is the kingdom of God governed by a whole new law, it also has an entirely different operating principle. Instead of operating by fear, this kingdom operates on faith. All who belong to it access its power and blessings by simple trust in the Father God and His Son Jesus Christ and in the promises of God as written in His Book—the Holy Bible.

The Choice Is Yours

Unlike the devil, who tries to force his will on those in his kingdom and to dominate them on every hand, God makes the people in His kingdom free. He is not a dictator. He does not force us to do His will. He does not even force us to live our lives by His operating principles. If we want to, we may submit ourselves again to the bondage of darkness, or we can walk in His liberty and light. It's our choice. Freedom to choose is a gift of God.

God says the same thing to us He said to the Israelites: "I have set before you life and death, blessing and cursing; therefore choose life, that both you and your descendants may live; that you may love the Lord your God, that you may obey His voice, and that you may cling to Him, for He is your life..." (Deut. 30:19, 20 NKJV). When you cling to Him, He clings to you.

Notice God not only listed our choices in that passage, but He also listed the consequence of each choice. If we choose to live His way and submit ourselves to the law of the Spirit of life in Christ Jesus, we will experience blessing. If we choose to live the devil's way and submit again to the bondage of sin and death, we will experience the curse. That's the law! You do not have a choice whether or not you live under spiritual law. It is like the law of gravity. It functions. However, you do get to choose the law of life or the law of death. This is a "no-brainer" decision. Who wants death and cursing when life and blessing are yours for the choosing?

We can choose our path but we cannot choose the consequences of that path. Those are already established.

We cannot have it both ways. We cannot live like the devil and enjoy the blessings of God. We can try, but it will never work. We're either going to be dedicated to God, living His way and being blessed, or we're going to be living like the world, overcome by sin and death.

What causes a Christian to live like the world even though it brings him trouble in the long run? The pressures of the flesh, the temptations of the devil, and short-term gratification. A Christian might see some attractive person and start stepping across moral boundaries, for example, disobeying the leading of God's Spirit and the teachings of God's Word. It might begin with just a little flirtation but end in adultery or fornication. He knows better. He cannot say, "The devil made me do it," because he is a believer.

He has been delivered from the devil's kingdom, and the devil does not have the power to make him sin. But he does it anyway because he wants to, all the while knowing it is wrong. That pressure is the lust or desire of the flesh.

It might seem fun for a while (sin can be pleasurable for a season), but then the consequences begin to catch up with him. Things start to go wrong. The destruction and death that are in the devil's kingdom begin to seep into that believer's life through the sinful choices he made. He wants relief from bad circumstances caused by disobedience without changing those circumstances, and he prays.

"God, I know You're a good God," he says. "Please pour out Your blessings in my life."

Do you know what the Bible says about that prayer from one who lives in disobedience? It doesn't reach the ear of God. That's right. Psalm 66:18 states clearly, "If I regard iniquity in my heart, the Lord will not hear me."

Does that mean God does not love that disobedient believer anymore? No. He still loves him as much as He ever did. But, as long as he is operating in the devil's kingdom—his ways of doing things—that Christian will reap the destructive results of the dark kingdom. God will not change it. It was not His choice or decision that produced the evil. The person chose his destiny. God gave him the freedom of choice: "If you are willing and obedient, you shall eat the good of the land; But if you refuse and rebel, you will be devoured by the sword. For the mouth of the Lord has spoken it" (Isa. 1:19, 20 AMP). But even when that person has disobeyed, God in His goodness will endeavor to get him back into the arena of obedience and blessing.

Personally, I have tried both ways. Before I was born again, I lived under the only law I knew, the law of sin and death. I lived there the first twenty years of my life and I despise it! I despise the devil and all of his works—sin, sickness, pain, poverty, fear, and disobedience. I have lived under the curse and I have lived under the blessing—there is no comparison. One is life. The other is death.

Before I gave my life to Jesus, I was under the devil's dominion and, being ignorant of God, I did not have any real choice. The only choice I knew was between bad and more bad. Now that I have been redeemed and made free by the law of the Spirit of life in Christ Jesus, I refuse to go back into the devil's bondage. I refuse to get over into the ways of darkness and fool around. I am not a creature of darkness anymore. I have been born again into the kingdom of light! The things in darkness have no appeal. I desire and enjoy love, peace, and joy.

God Will Teach You

"But, Gloria," you might say, "what if I don't know what the Lord wants me to do? What if I don't know much about His ways?" Give Him some of your time and attention, and He will teach you! Psalm 25 says:

> Good and upright is the Lord; therefore He teaches sinners in the way. The humble He guides in justice, and the humble He teaches His way.... Who is the man that fears the Lord? Him shall He teach in the way He chooses. He himself shall dwell in prosperity, and his descendants shall

inherit the earth. The secret of the Lord is with those who fear Him, and He will show them His covenant.

vv. 8, 9, 12–14 NKJV

God is so good that even when you're off course, even when you're still a sinner, He will teach you His ways to get you back on course. That's how we got into His kingdom in the first place! He began to open the eyes of our heart and teach us the truth. He showed us that we were sinners and needed a Savior. Then He taught us—probably through the Bible, a preacher, or a believing friend—that Jesus, the Son of God, lived and died and rose again to become the Savior we need.

Once we gave our lives to Him, God not only made His written Word available to us, He put His own Holy Spirit in our hearts to teach us exactly how to apply that Word to our lives. John 14:26 says He will teach us "all things"! Did you know that you can have a faith class any time you want? Did you know you can tune in to the teaching of the Holy Spirit any hour of the day or night and find out what God wants you to do because He is living in your heart? The Israelites in Old Testament times could not do that. They had to have an anointed person—a rabbi, prophet, or priest—to teach them what God was saying to them. They didn't have hearts that could hear the voice of the Lord. They didn't have His Spirit within them to give them light. We are a blessed people! We have the Lord Himself to teach us His ways. As we saw earlier in Psalm 25:13, if we will walk in those ways when God shows them to us, we will "dwell in prosperity," we will "lodge in goodness." That's a wonderful place to live, don't you think?

What's more, I can take that blessed environment with me

wherever I go! It's not tied to a particular location. It's not tied to circumstances. It's in my heart and my relationship with the Lord. God's goodness surrounds me wherever I go.

The Living Bible confirms that: "Where is the man who fears the Lord? God will teach him how to choose the best. He shall live within God's circle of blessing" (vv. 12, 13). I love that phrase *the circle of blessing.* It tells me that when I am paying attention to the Lord and obeying His voice, whichever way I turn, there is a blessing. I have a circle of blessing around me. So if I go to one place, that circle goes with me and keeps me surrounded by God's goodness. If I go to another place, the circle goes with me there. I could go to the deepest, darkest jungle or the meanest place in the world, and when I arrived, I would still be encompassed by God's circle of blessing! The circle of blessing is His presence crowning and surrounding me with lovingkindness and tender mercies:

> Bless the Lord, O my soul: and all that is within me, bless his holy name. Bless the Lord, O my soul, and forget not all his benefits: who forgiveth all thine iniquities; who healeth all thy diseases; who redeemeth thy life from destruction; who crowneth thee with lovingkindness and tender mercies,
>
> Psalm 103:1–4

Early in our Christian life, before Ken and I understood these things, we found out what can happen when you step outside the circle of blessing by disobeying the Lord. We were struggling financially and having no success in life. God had spoken to both of us in our hearts and told us that He wanted us to move to Tulsa, Oklahoma, so that Ken could enroll in Oral Roberts University.

We could think of several good reasons why we shouldn't do that. After all, he was thirty years old—who wants to be a thirty-year-old freshman? What's more, we didn't have the money for the tuition or anything else and we had small children. We didn't know how we would make ends meet. To tell you the truth, at this time in our lives we did not know much of anything about God and how He works. So we didn't follow the leading of the Lord.

We disobeyed Him, stayed right where we were, and things got worse...and worse...and worse.

The longer we disregarded God's direction, the further out of His will we got until finally we hit some real trouble. We had a bad car wreck that seriously endangered our lives. We knew the wreck was the result of being out of the will of God. With God's help and mercy, we became willing to move to Tulsa and obey God's direction concerning ORU.

Some people might say, "God must have done that. He sent that car wreck to get your attention."

No, God did not send the car wreck. It was not in His will for us. We had to get out of His will to find it. We had to get out of God's territory and by ignorance or disobedience get into the devil's territory to be vulnerable to something like that.

God was not our problem, but He was surely our answer. In fact, He is never the problem. People often assume when horrible things happen that God caused them. They assume that since He is God, He always has His way. But He does not always have His way in people's lives. Bible history is full of people He did not have His way with—including Adam. He will ultimately have His way in His overall plan for the earth, but He will not force people to take part in that plan. He will do everything He can do to reach them. He will send angels to help them. He will send witnesses to them. He will reveal things to them. But if they reject Him and go their own way, He will allow them to do it even though it's going to get them in trouble.

Then, most of the time, they point their finger at Him and say, "God, why did You let this happen to me?"

He didn't do it to them... they did it to themselves!

Somebody might say, "Well, if God is so good, why didn't He bless them anyway?" Because God's goodness prevents Him from blessing something that's wrong even if He loves the person who is doing it. He has already said, "If you trust and obey Me, you will be blessed. If you don't, you will be cursed." He keeps His Word. You can count on the fact that if He tells you to go one way and you continue to go the opposite way, things are going to get bad for you. You are in the wrong place. You are out of your circle of blessing.

God is a good God and He gives us every opportunity to receive that goodness, but nobody who lives a life of disobedience is ever blessed. Jeremiah 32:19 NKJV says about God, "You are great in counsel and mighty in work, for your eyes are open to all the ways of the sons of men, to give everyone according to his ways and according to the fruit of his doings." Thank God for the blood of Jesus and the mercy of God that enables us to repent and receive God's forgiveness so we don't have to reap the negative consequences of our ways. But we need to understand if we continue in a lifestyle of disobedience, we are going to eat some very bitter fruit.

Ken and I found out just how true that was when we had the

car wreck. So we jumped back into the plan of God as quickly as we could. We got ourselves into the center of His will where we could be surrounded by His goodness and His blessings, really for the first time in our lives. Sure enough, things began to work for us. All our problems did not disappear overnight, but they began to get better immediately. God's kingdom law of increase started operating in our lives and began to whittle away the mountain of financial debt we had accumulated. Even though for some time Ken was in school and was only working part time as a pilot for Oral Roberts, we were debt free in eleven months! (We did that by beginning to learn and obey what God says about money.)

It wasn't easy, but it happened as we obeyed the Lord.

Resisting the Enemy

There is one thing I want to make perfectly clear. I am not saying that every Christian who runs into trouble is somehow in disobedience to the Lord. There are wonderful believers who love the Lord and live good, godly lives and yet they experience tragic things. Why is that? As I said at the beginning of this chapter, it is because God is not the only one at work in the earth. The Bible does not say you will not have any trouble, but it does say over and over that God will bring you out of trouble. It also says, "The just shall live by faith" (Rom. 1:17). When trouble comes, faith in God's Word will bring victory. First John 5:4 says, "For whatsoever is born of God overcometh the world: and this is the victory that overcometh the world, even our faith."

We have an enemy. He comes to steal, kill, and destroy. We have authority over him in the Name of Jesus, but even so, he will challenge us to see if we will really use that authority against him. He will try to frighten us with negative circumstances so that he can gain entrance into our lives.

First Peter 5:8 NKJV warns us about him, saying, "Be sober, be vigilant; because your adversary the devil walks about like a roaring lion, seeking whom he may devour."

There is a battle between light and darkness in this world. The devil will do bad things to good people if he can get away with it. He is a thief and is always endeavoring to steal God's blessings from us. Although we enjoy a great deal of protection from him simply by avoiding sin and living in obedience to the Word of God, we cannot ever afford to just sit back complacently and think we're immune from the devil's attacks.

We have to be spiritually aggressive. As Jesus said, "The kingdom of heaven suffereth violence, and the violent take it by force" (Matt. 11:12). If we want to enjoy all the blessings of God's kingdom that belong to us, we have to find out what they are and then take hold of them by faith and receive them. What God offers has to be received. When the devil tries to harm us or take those blessings away, we must resist him with "the sword of the Spirit, which is the word of God" (Eph. 6:17). We have to resist Satan's lies and influence.

Think again about the operating principles of the two kingdoms. The kingdom of God operates by faith. The kingdom of the devil operates by fear. If we want to operate in God's kingdom, we must live by faith. Romans 10:17 says faith comes by hearing the Word. We have to continually renew our mind with God's Word (Rom. 12:1, 2). We can only believe in faith what we know He has said. We must be willing to keep believing what God says even when circumstances tell a different story. Second Corinthians 5:67 tells us that while we are in this body, "we walk by faith, not by sight." We must believe God is good in every situation and resist the fear and doubt the devil tries to bring.

If you are afraid of storms, for example, you must fill your heart with God's promises of protection until that fear is forced out of your heart and the peace of God takes its place. Then, when a storm comes your way, your heart and your mouth will be filled with faith. You can stop the devil in his tracks and that storm won't be able to harm you. Faith-filled words dominate the laws of sin and death.

The Safest Place on Earth

If you have not studied the scriptural promises God has given His people, the idea of being protected from a storm may surprise you. You may not have realized that the kingdom of heaven guarantees physical as well as spiritual safety for its citizens, even while they are living on this war-torn earth.

There are many verses in the Bible that speak of that protection, but none is better than Psalm 91. It reveals how two kingdoms exist side by side on the earth. One is fraught with the danger, disease, death, and destruction the devil brings. The other provides perfect protection, peace, and the goodness of God. This is such an amazing psalm, I encourage you to read it right now all the way through:

He that dwelleth in the secret place of the most High shall
abide under the shadow of the Almighty. I will say of the Lord,

He is my refuge and my fortress: my God; in him will I trust. Surely he shall deliver thee from the snare of the fowler, and from the noisome pestilence. He shall cover thee with his feathers, and under his wings shalt thou trust: his truth shall be thy shield and buckler. Thou shalt not be afraid for the terror by night; nor for the arrow that flieth by day; nor for the pestilence that walketh in darkness; nor for the destruction that wasteth at noonday. A thousand shall fall at thy side, and ten thousand at thy right hand; but it shall not come nigh thee. Only with thine eyes shalt thou behold and see the reward of the wicked. Because thou hast made the Lord, which is my refuge, even the most High, thy habitation; there shall no evil befall thee, neither shall any plague come nigh thy dwelling. For he shall give his angels charge over thee, to keep thee in all thy ways. They shall bear thee up in their hands, lest thou dash thy foot against a stone. Thou shalt tread upon the lion and adder: the young lion and the dragon shalt thou trample under feet. Because he hath set his love upon me, therefore will I deliver him: I will set him on high, because he hath known my name. He shall call upon me, and I will answer him: I will be with him in trouble; I will deliver him, and honour him. With long life will I satisfy him, and show him my salvation.

Look again at the first verse of this psalm, and you will see these guarantees of safety do not apply to the man or woman who goes in and out of the will of God. They're not promised to those who call themselves Christians but live like the world. They are for those who abide in God, those who consistently endeavor to hear and obey His voice.

Some time ago, the Lord spoke to my heart as I woke up and said, *Separate yourself and you will be separated.* Then He reminded me of the scripture that says, "Come out from among them, and be ye separate, saith the Lord, and touch not the unclean thing; and I will receive you, and will be a Father unto you, and ye shall be my sons and daughters" (2 Cor. 6:17).

I knew what the Lord was telling me. He was reminding me that if I will separate myself from darkness, sin, and evil and live for Him, He will separate me from the danger and destructive events that are taking place around me. I'll be able to live safely even in dangerous times and places.

Somebody might ask, "Do you really believe that?"

Yes, I really do. I have seen the fruit of it in my life. A few years ago, my little granddaughter Lyndsey contracted one of the most deadly forms of meningitis. By the time my daughter and son-in-law got her to the hospital, she was unconscious and in critical condition. Several children in the city had already died of it, and the doctors told us that the next twenty-four hours would determine whether Lyndsey would live or die.

All our family members—even the little ones—know about the protection of God, so every one of us stood our ground. We refused to fear despite the terrible reports the doctors were giving us. Kellie, her mother, said in powerful faith as she heard the life-threatening doctor's report, "I REFUSE TO FEAR." She said the fear that shrouded her as the doctor spoke just lifted off her and was never able to return. She was geared up for the fight of faith over life and death. We resisted the devil's attempt to steal our kingdom blessings, and by faith we said, "Lyndsey will live and not die." At the first sign of trouble, we all go into victory mode!

We won! After about ten hours, Lyndsey regained conscious-ness. Even before she regained full consciousness, her first words to her grandfather were, "PaPa, by Jesus' stripes I am healed!" That word from God was in her spirit.

The devil tried to steal that little girl from our family, but we stood fast on the goodness of the Lord. We didn't wring our hands and say, "Well, I'm just scared to death. What if Lyndsey doesn't pull through?" No, we said words like Psalm 91, "The Lord is our refuge and our fortress. We trust in Him and refuse to fear! Deadly pestilence shall not come near our dwelling. He shall cover us with His wings and under His wings we do trust. His Word is our shield and buckler."[7]

There is a song that says, "Whose report will you believe?" And then it answers, "I shall believe the report of the Lord!" That is exactly what we did. That song is inspired by Isaiah 53:3–6, which reveals to us that healing already belongs to us. All we have to do is receive the report that Jesus bore our sicknesses, weak-nesses, and pains at the same time He bore our sins. He took the whole curse of sin into Himself. He did it for Lyndsey. He did it for you! He did it for me! It is a higher report than the doctor's report. It is God's report. The Copeland family always believes God's report.[8]

---

7. Luke 21:11—In *The Amplified Bible,* it says pestilences are "plagues: malig-nant and contagious or infectious epidemic diseases which are deadly and dev-astating." To learn more about how to keep victory in your family, see Kellie Copeland Kutz's book *Protecting Your Family in Dangerous Times* (Harrison House, 2002).

8. For more understanding of how to receive healing, read *God's Will for You* by Gloria Copeland.

We refused to let fear in, and we moved and spoke with faith in the Word of God.

Thanks to the lovingkindness of the Lord, Lyndsey is alive and well today with a beautiful life yet to live! To God be the glory.

I could sit here and write for hours about the times the Lord has protected us from danger. I remember a trip I made to Israel when I was staying in one of the most dangerous areas of the country. At that time, the enemy had recently raided the very kibbutz, or settlement, we were visiting. One night as I lay down to sleep on the little slab that served as my bed, I thought, *What if they raid tonight?*

My very next thought was Psalm 91. I rehearsed its promises of protection in my mind, then I turned over and went to sleep, secure in the knowledge that I was in the kingdom of God—the safest place on earth.

Any Time, Any Place, in Any Situation

Because they don't understand how much spiritual things affect this natural earth, most people assume the results in their lives are determined by their natural environment, resources, and circumstances. But the truth is, the blessings (or lack of them) in our lives are determined by the spiritual kingdom in which we are operating. I've seen it demonstrated over and over again. God can protect and prosper anyone who will give his life to Him and walk in His ways—and He can do it any time, any place, in any economy.

A story we printed years ago in our ministry magazine perfectly illustrated this fact. It told of a village in southwest Africa where there had been a severe drought for almost ten years. People were starving in the whole region surrounding the village. It was in awful shape. The reservoir had been empty so long, the dam was crumbling and broken.

But the Lord told the pastor to have the church members fix the dam by faith. Do you know what happened? It rained. The little reservoir filled up. The believers planted their gardens next to the unbelievers' gardens all around the reservoir. The believers prayed and trusted God to bless the fruit of their ground. The unbelievers, of course, did not.

The results? Not only did the believers' gardens outproduce the others, yielding more than twice the normal harvest during the normal growing season, their gardens kept producing the whole year long! He used those gardens to provide a miraculous sign and confirm the truth that Jesus is Lord.[9]

You might live in a town where the economy has dried up. Nobody there may be prospering. But, if you are born of God and you are walking in obedience to Him, it doesn't matter if there is any money in your town or not—God will still bless you. You belong to Him. There is money in the kingdom of God!

A letter we received from a minister in Sierra Leone verifies that. He wrote:

Dear Brother and Sister Copeland,

Prior to 1986, we were very religious and believed that poverty was a spiritual way of life. My denomination at that time paid me less than one U.S. dollar a month. I was married

---

9. "A Winter Harvest," *Believer's Voice of Victory,* Vol. 17, No. 11, 1989.

with a child and could not afford food for my family or rent for my home. Then we listened to your teachings from the Fire Conference in Zimbabwe and began to teach that revelation. I quit that denomination and God launched what we're doing now. We've been blessed ever since. God's faithfulness has put food on the table, given us a car, and our ministry and our members are prospering. The opposition is silenced and we are marked as a prosperity gospel church. We are seeing God save, heal, and deliver souls.

S. B.

Sierra Leone

You can be in the most dire circumstances and still prosper, because your prosperity doesn't come from the world; it comes from the kingdom of God. Certainly, God can, and usually does, use natural situations to bring that blessing to you. But it's the laws of His kingdom that are at work causing those natural situations to come together. Then again, He is not limited to the natural circumstances. All things are possible with God, and all things are possible to him that believeth!

Ken and I minister on television in many financially barren nations. Several years ago I was told that in one particular city our broadcast reaches, there were no dogs left. The people had eaten them all.

Yet at the same time, we received one letter after another from people in the same nation telling us how God was increasing them. The whole nation was suffering a housing shortage, yet the members of a family who gave their lives to the Lord and began believing God's report were offered a much better place even though their housing was dictated by the government. People got jobs when no one else around them could find any work. God is good. His Word believed and acted on will work anywhere. He is a provision-giving God, and He has the capacity and willingness to come to the aid of anyone who will receive from Him in faith.

If you are a citizen of the kingdom of God, all things are possible to you no matter where you live. God is not dependent on governments and methods of men. He will intervene and use those things, but He is not restricted by them. He has the power to get you what you need any time, any place, and in any situation.

I heard a wonderful testimony along those lines from a couple that ministers in Ireland. They were living in another country when they gave their lives to the Lord and attended a church there for some time. Although they both had jobs with the government, they began to sense the Lord leading them into full-time ministry. They felt they were to start a work for the Lord in Ireland, but they could not figure out how they would get the money. In the natural they couldn't afford to quit their jobs, much less start a ministry in another nation. They were believing God to make a way where there was no way.

One day, they received news that their government had decided to decrease the number of government employees by offering any employee that had been a civil servant for a certain number of years the opportunity to resign and receive five years' salary at the time of their resignation. This couple responded immediately and signed up for that program.

Shortly thereafter, the government discontinued the program because it became clear that it was financially unwise. As it turned out, this couple were the only ones who got in on it before it was revoked! They got their money and moved to Ireland.

Clearly, when God's kingdom comes on the scene, even natural, worldly systems begin to work in favor of the believer. If you'll honor and obey Him, you can live in the light of His goodness right in the midst of a dark world. You will begin to experience increase. In a world plagued by shortages and lack, you'll find He is able to "supply all your need according to his riches in glory by Christ Jesus" (Phil. 4:19).[10]

10. To learn more about the blessing of God to increase financially, read *The Laws of Prosperity* by Kenneth Copeland and *God's Will Is Prosperity* by Gloria Copeland.

CHAPTER 7

The Key to Heaven's Storehouse

But seek ye first the kingdom of God, and his righteousness;
and all these things shall be added unto you.

MATTHEW 6:33

Once we realize God has a storehouse of good things laid up for us and we decide to plant ourselves firmly in His kingdom so that we qualify for those blessings, the first question we want to ask is this: What can I do to open the door to God's storehouse so I can begin receiving the good things God has for me?

In Matthew 6:24–33 NKJV Jesus gives us the answer:

No one can serve two masters; for either he will hate the one and love the other, or else he will be loyal to the one and despise the other. You cannot serve God and mammon. Therefore I say to you, do not worry about your life, what you will eat or what you will drink; nor about your body, what you will put on. Is not life more than food and the body more than clothing? Look at the birds of the air, for they neither sow nor reap nor gather into barns; yet your heavenly Father feeds them. Are you not of more value than they? Which of you by worrying can add one cubit to his stature? So why do you worry about clothing? Consider the lilies of the field, how they grow: they neither toil nor spin; and yet I say to you that even Solomon in all his glory was not arrayed like one of these. Now if God so clothes the grass of the field, which today is, and tomorrow is thrown into the oven, will He not much more clothe you, O you of little faith? Therefore do not worry, saying, "What shall we eat?" or "What shall we drink?" or "What shall we wear?" For after all these things the Gentiles seek. For your heavenly Father knows that you need all these things. But seek first the kingdom of God and His righteousness, and all these things shall be added to you.

Jesus tells us that God's way to gain natural provision and prosperity is as different from the worldly way of gaining those things as day is from night. The world teaches us to make material wealth our goal. It teaches us to focus on and pursue the money we need to buy the things we want. It teaches us to connive and scheme, to do whatever it takes to get ahead.

But God instructs us to do just the opposite. He tells us not to focus on material riches. Instead, seek Him first and trust Him to supply our needs. He says, *Don't push and strive to gain material riches for yourself. Serve Me and I'll give them to you.*

In other words, God is our source. One of my favorite examples of how faithfully God meets the needs of those who put Him first in their lives is the experience of Grandma Martha. Although she wasn't my own grandmother, she was the grandmother of a friend of mine, and I've heard my friend tell stories about her. This is how she described Grandma's life.

My mother's parents died when she and her brothers and sisters were younger, so Grandma Martha raised them. You've got to understand that she didn't have a job. She took in washing or whatever she could find to do. There were times when she didn't have food for the children. My mom said that Grandma Martha walked around all through the day while she was cleaning and dusting, and she would stop and say, "I know that You know and You know that I know that You know. So I just want to remind You that I know that You know." And then one evening about 6 o'clock, somebody knocked on the door and said, "Ms. Martha, God told me to bring you a bushel of groceries." It was enough to feed the children all week. This is just one of the stories.

There was another time in the dead of winter when it was very, very cold. She had burned all the coal that they had. The children were wearing their coats inside the house. She had even begun to break up little furnishings to keep warm, but the fire was getting lower and lower. Grandma Martha would walk all through the day and say, "I just want You to know that I know that You know. And I just want to remind You that I know that You know and it's all right." A truck pulled up in the back of the yard before dark. It was a coal truck. The man never even got out. He just released the lever and put enough coal in the yard to last them all winter.

Every morning Grandma Martha would wake up at 4 o'clock and visit with the Lord. She would say to Him, "God, I have a covenant with You, and I thank You for saving my children and their children and their children and their children. They will serve You, and they will honor You." Then she would take out her Bible and read scriptures to the Lord. After that she had a praise and worship service, just by herself, singing and praising the Lord and worshiping Him.

When she finished she would reach down for her purse and look through it for money. My mother said that sometimes she would just find one little penny. That was all she had in her purse. She took that little penny or that nickel or whatever she found and put it on the table to offer it unto the Lord. Every morning at 4 o'clock, Grandma Martha prayed and made an offering unto the Lord.

It is said that when Grandmother walked into church, she would say, "Everything dead ought to be resurrected. I came to praise the Lord; I came to lift up and glorify His Name. My eyes are lifted up to the hills from whence cometh my help." She came in talking and praising God. My soul magnifies the Lord because I had a grandmother who had a relationship with God.

When Grandma Martha got ready to go be with the Lord, she was way up in her 90's, and her sight began to fail. One of my relatives came over to see her and he said, "Ms. Martha, I just came to visit with you today." She was lying on the bed, and this relative didn't know that Grandma's sight had left her. Grandma reached down on the side of the bed and began to feel for her shoe. She could sense her relative watching her, and she said, "Brother Bill, don't worry about me because I see what you don't see. It's all right because I am getting ready to go be with the Lord. My soul is well." She lived by faith, and she died by faith.

One day Grandma Martha was preparing to go be with

the Lord. My aunts were in the yard hanging out clothes, and they heard her talking in her room. They wondered, *Who is Grandma talking to?* They came into the room, and Grandma was talking to an angel.

My aunt said, "Grandma, who are you talking to?" She said, "Don't you see that chariot over there in the corner? There's a golden chariot there and a man standing there. He is waiting for me. And I just finished telling him that if he would just bring it a little lower, I'm gonna step on there."

My auntie began to cry and say, "Grandma, Grandma, don't leave us. Grandma, don't leave us." She said, "Hush, child. Don't you know this ain't Grandma's home? Grandma didn't come here to stay always. Grandma's got another home that's not made by man." They sat in there with Grandma hoping they could keep her from going to be with the Lord. Grandma wouldn't say anything. She just lay there and smiled.

Right before she went to be with the Lord, Grandma stopped eating. She fasted. She wouldn't drink water and wouldn't eat food. They couldn't even put it in her mouth. She was fasting and singing and praising, giving glory and worship to the Lord. That evening Grandma stepped on that chariot, and it took her home to be with the Lord.

I know my grandmother is standing up there, and she is one of that cloud of witnesses that is cheering me on saying, "Go, Carolyn. Go for it. I prayed you in here. This is that covenant that I didn't stay to see, but I had faith in God that it would come to pass." You see, even when I was in sin and an alcoholic drinking a fifth of Scotch every day and taking all kinds of dope, my grandma's prayers were circling the earth.

Those prayers began a Holy Ghost rope that roped me by the neck and dragged me into the kingdom of God.

Grandmother had a relationship with God, and she offered unto Him all that she had and all that she was. She offered Him a living sacrifice.

Naturally speaking, Grandma Martha had many opportunities to be anxious and "take thought" about what she and the children were going to eat or what they were going to wear. There were times when she faced needs that she had no earthly way of meeting. During those times she trusted God with her life and the lives of her children and grandchildren through four generations. God met her needs!

Of course, that was not God's best for Grandma Martha. His desire was to prosper and bless her with abundance. But she didn't know that. Because she thought His will was only to supply her with the most basic provisions, that was as far as her faith went. So she walked in all the light she had, depending on God and honoring Him. She trusted Him to meet her needs. He faithfully and supernaturally met her expectation, always seeing to it that her needs were met. Grandma was far ahead of most Christians of her day. What she lacked in knowledge was more than offset by her dedication and faithfulness! She gave herself to God. That is the greatest offering of all!

She trusted God in death the same as she did in life. What a testimony she left behind.

I wanted to share Grandma Martha with you because her story has always blessed and inspired me. It will be great fun to meet her one day. Don't you know her mansion will be marvelous to visit!

Now, you don't have to be a poor, uneducated grandmother to

live in that kind of dependence on God. You can be a brain surgeon and live that way. If, as a brain surgeon, you will put God first place in your life and focus on Him instead of focusing all your life and efforts on becoming a success, then God will bless you in your work and make you more successful than you ever could have been without Him. If you'll seek God first, when you begin an operation, the wisdom and power of God will be there to help you. He knows things about brain surgery nobody else knows!

I know of at least one case in which a brain surgeon who trusted God in his life encountered a situation during surgery that could have turned out very badly if the Lord had not helped him. The surgeon thought he knew exactly what to do and was about to make a cut to remove a tumor when, suddenly, the Spirit of the Lord prompted him to stop and do it differently. Afterward, he realized there was more to the situation than he knew. If he had continued with the standard procedure, the patient would have died. But because he depended on the Lord, the patient lived and fully recovered!

More Than a One-Time Event

Since Matthew 6:33 is the key that opens the door to our storehouse of blessings, we need to know exactly what it means to "seek first the kingdom of God." Webster's dictionary tells us the word *seek* means "to try to find, to search for, to look for, to go to, to resort to, to search, to explore, to ask, to inquire for, to try to learn or discern." It denotes diligent inquiry.

The Hebrew word for *seek* (*doresh*) gives us even more insight. It comes from the root word that means "to tread or frequent." In Hebrew *seek* means "to ask, diligently inquire, require or search."

Therefore, "seek first the kingdom of God" would mean to tread frequently or walk continually in pursuit of God, following after or searching out His ways of thinking and doing. Rabbi Isidor Zwirn, in his book *The Rabbi From Burbank,* said this about the word *doresh* translated "seek" in our English Bible:

Research (*doresh*) with integrity equals knowledge and insight. Knowledge and insight, plus obedience, equals God's rich rewards. When I learn to *know* what God is saying to me in his Word, I must *obey* what he says. Then he is honor-bound to answer the promises in His Word.

So, once a student dedicated himself to the twin virtues of research *and* obedience, he soon learned to recognize God's scriptural commands as he read them. A few of these I have translated literally from the Hebrew:

"Research (*doresh*) Yehovah and his strength; seek his face eternally" (1 Chronicles 16:11). If I am to entrust myself to God, I must be aware of what it means. And if I learn for myself of his strength, his power, his might, then I can confidently relax in his care.

"Research (*doresh*) Yehovah if you are to find him. Call upon him, for he is always near" (Isaiah 55:6). How wonderful to know that he is available, and that when we seek (research) for Him in His Word, that we will find him, "for he is always near."

"Those who know thy name will trust thee, for thou hast not forsaken them who research (*doresh*) thee, Yehovah" (Psalm 9:11). How does one come to know his name? By study, by research.

"I researched (*doresh*) Yehovah and he answered me, and from all my confusions he saved me" (Psalm 34:5). What a promise! When I sought him through his Word, he readily responded to my urgent needs! *Baruch ha Shem!* Praise his Name!

"Those who research (*doresh*) Yehovah will never lack the goodness of life" (Psalm 34:11). How can anyone say that our great God is not interested in the most intimate details of our lives? Or that he is not concerned about such "mundane" things as our food, clothing, and shelter?

"When the meek saw they became glad. Those who will research (*doresh*) Yehovah, their (dead) hearts will be made alive" (Psalm 69:33). Again, in addition to our physical well-being, God is interested in our emotional wellbeing. He wants us to be glad, happy, and vibrant with his joy and his peace. All this and more he promises to all his children, when we seek, research, study, and *know* him through his Word.

"I never cease to be amazed as I look at these references and the scores of others like them. God evidently expects us to seek him with all of our powers. When we do, we have his Word that we will "find" him and "know" Him. Of course, the connotation in this finding and knowing is that we will then offer ourselves to him in total obedience."[11]

In other words, seeking God is not a one-time event. It's a life-style of going after God and His ways. This is exactly how we

---

11. Zwirn, Isidor, *The Rabbi From Burbank,* 1986 Tyndale House Publishers, Inc., Wheaton, Ill.

learned to study and meditate the Word of God. Just reading is not a description of feeding—partaking of, receiving, living God's Word.

Researching God and His ways in order to obey them gives great insight on how to develop a victorious and overcoming life. I loved Rabbi Zwirn's book so much we put it back into print. It is a wealth of wisdom!

Some people think that just because they gave their lives to the Lord at one time, that makes them God-seekers. But they are mistaken. Even if that one-time event does qualify them for entry into heaven when they die, it will not guarantee a blessed and productive life on this earth. The initial experience of being born again must be followed by a lifetime of walking with Him in order to lead a blessed and productive life.

If we seek first the kingdom of God, we will do more than just go to church on Sunday. (Although that's a good start!) We will frequent God's throne of grace through times of prayer. We will continually research and obey His Word. We will go often to places where we can fellowship with other believers and worship in Jesus' Name.

Just how frequently must we do those things to qualify as a diligent seeker?

Christianity is not a religion based on law but a relationship based on the heart, so there is no hard and fast answer to that question. But if we look back at Matthew 6, it will point us in the right direction. It says that those who do not know the Lord "diligently seek" natural provision for their lives (v. 32 AMP).

One thing you can say for unbelievers, they diligently seek worldly things! If you want to see what it means to diligently seek something, watch how most people get up every morning and go to work so they can get that paycheck. They go whether they want to or not. They go rain or shine. They go whether they like their job or whether they don't.

Why? Because they want to have something to eat and something to wear and something to drive!

I have found that believers who truly seek the Lord first are as diligent about spending time with Him as ordinary people are about going to work every day. They love and enjoy Him and desire to spend time with Him. He is their source of life and blessing. Every good thing in their lives comes from Him. They are dependent on Him the way the world is dependent on their paycheck.

Does that mean they don't bother to go to work every day? No, God-seeking believers are as diligent as unbelievers in their work, and should be more so. But their motivation is different. They don't go to work just so they can get a paycheck. They go to work because that's what the Lord tells them to do in His Word and they want to obey Him. Ephesians 4:28 says, "Let him that stole steal no more: but rather let him labour, working with his hands the thing which is good, that he may have to give to him that needeth."

The most important way to seek God first is to spend time with Him every day in His Word and in prayer. I like to pray in the morning before I begin the rest of my day. Usually, that is when I do my Bible study, too. I learn so much during those times. Oh, how I love the time I spend in the mornings fellowshiping with Him!

Of course, I really put my heart into my time with God. I don't just sit down and read my Bible because it's my religious duty. I like to use several translations, especially the *King James Version, The Amplified Bible*, and *The New Living Translation*. I might read a passage of Scripture in these translations and then get out my *Companion Bible*, a study Bible that has excellent comments and insights by E. W. Bullinger.[12] I'll see what the remarks are on the verses I read. Sometimes that Bible will tell me what the original language said or give me some other, related scriptures to read. I love the wisdom of God! I greatly enjoy the Hebrew commentaries by historical Jewish scholars. They give so much insight.

I enjoy myself so much and get so interested going from one reference to the other that sometimes I want to say, "Help! I've started studying and I can't stop!" What am I doing during these times? I am seeking, researching the wisdom of my Father, the God of creation. How exciting can life be!

Although I often preach about the things I see during those times of fellowship, I've never been able to share all the insight I gain when it's just the Lord and me.

You might say, "Well, I like to learn about the Word by listening to preaching tapes."

So do I! That's very important. CDs and tapes are such a blessing, and it is very beneficial to listen to them throughout your day whenever you can. But the fact is, you cannot get all you need from the Lord just by listening to someone else. The time you spend alone with Him is what really makes the difference. You take what you learn from others and let God add to it exactly what you need. You will never live fully in the goodness of God until you learn how to fellowship with Him alone.

In addition to spending time with the Lord in prayer and feeding your spirit with His Word, you put God first by taking one day at a time and living for God. You do what He shows you to do that day. You listen to the Holy Spirit whom God has sent to you as teacher

---

12. *The Companion Bible, King James Version*, Originally published in 1922, Notes and Appendixes by E. W. Bullinger (Grand Rapids: Kregel Publications, 2000).

and guide. When situations arise and you have a choice either to handle them God's way or the world's way, you choose God's way. Obedience is required in putting God first place in your life.

When you seek God first, you let Him be God in every area of your life. You give yourself to Him out of honor, reverence, and love. You make a decision: "All right, Lord, I'll do whatever You tell me to do. I'm giving You the rest of my days on this earth— starting today." Then you let God be God in your life. He's the first One you believe. He's the first One you obey.

Look again at Matthew 6:33 in *The Amplified Bible:* "But seek (aim at and strive after) first of all His kingdom and His righteousness (His way of doing and being right), and then all these things taken together will be given you besides."

"His kingdom and His righteousness, (His way of doing and being right)" is very easy to understand. Seek first the way God does things. Another way the Bible says this is "walk in his ways" (Deut. 8:6; 10:12; 11:22; 26:17; 28:9; 30:16, etc.). Be diligent and seek to know God's ways—what He says is right. Pattern after His ways of doing and being right. It takes more than a lifetime to know all about God. But from the moment you begin to seek and follow what you learn about Him, your life will begin to improve. The more you seek, the more you obey what you discover about God's way of doing things, the more your life is lived in days of heaven upon the earth.

Deuteronomy 28:1–2 says:

> And it shall come to pass, if thou shalt hearken diligently unto the voice of the Lord thy God, to observe and to do all his commandments which I command thee this day, that the Lord thy God will set thee on high above all nations of the earth:

And all these blessings shall come on thee, and overtake thee,
if thou shalt hearken unto the voice of the Lord thy God.

If people around you—your family or friends—tell you something that contradicts God's Word, you don't listen to them. You listen to Him instead because He is Number One. He comes first—before yourself, before your family, before your career, before anything else in your life. There's no one else as important to you as He is. Let God have the final word! He is always right.

Some people think their family is supposed to come first. Family is important, but they cannot bring you salvation. They cannot bring the power and blessings of heaven down on your life. If you will put God first, however, and go after His kingdom and way of doing things, your family will benefit from it. You'll be a better spouse to your husband or wife. You'll be a better parent to your children. Your home will be filled with the love and peace of God instead of strife and confusion. By seeking God first, you will put your family in a position to enjoy the goodness of God.

As you first begin to get to know the Lord and His ways of doing things, your understanding is limited. You may only know a few things He wants you to do, and that's okay. Just obey Him in those things and seek (research) to know more. As you gradually increase in the knowledge of Him, the level of His blessing in your life will increase too! He will just keep adding more and more of Himself and good things to you! The speed with which this happens will depend upon the diligence with which you seek after Him.

Some people are reluctant to put God first place because they are afraid of what He might tell them to do. They are afraid to seek Him because they don't know what they will find.

If that is how you feel, let me assure you, there is nothing to fear. When you seek God first, what you will find is His goodness and His blessings. Even if He tells you something that seems hard on your flesh, you will be glad you obeyed Him because that obedience will open the door to good for you. God's will always adds to you. It does not take from you.

When I first began to live for the Lord, if I could have looked forward forty years to where I am now, it would have been much easier for me to follow His direction for my life. If I had known then how good God is, I wouldn't have hesitated for a moment to do anything He asked me to do.

Looking back, I can tell you not only from the Scriptures but from my own experience, and the experiences of others, that "the Lord is good...to the soul that seeketh Him" (Lam. 3:25). His dream is to have people who will let Him be God in their lives so He can richly bless them and demonstrate His goodness to the world, through them. He has never been stingy toward His people. The Bible tells us that our heavenly Father knows exactly what we need—spirit, soul, body, financially, and socially. He knows and He delights in meeting those needs. He wants us to be complete, with nothing missing and nothing broken.

He wants us to have the best of the best, but He can only give it to us if we seek Him first.

Pursue Him with Passion

There is another quality that marks true, scriptural seeking in addition to diligence. It's an attitude of wholehearted passion that verges on desperation. Real seekers don't just go after the things of God casually, when it's convenient. They go after Him as if they cannot live without Him. They seek Him, as *The Amplified Bible* says, out of "vital necessity."

A real seeker acts like the woman Jesus spoke of in Luke 15 who lost one of her ten silver coins. She lit a lamp and swept her house late into the night searching for it. Then, when she found it, she called "her friends and neighbors together, saying, 'Rejoice with me, for I have found the piece which I lost!'" (Luke 15:9 NKJV).

I can identify with that woman because I've lost my car keys too often. Ken says, "Gloria, if you'd put your keys in the same place every day, you wouldn't have to hunt for them." (But I don't take time to put them in the same place every day. I'm a busy person!) So my need to go somewhere has often begun with a feverish search for my keys. I'll turn the house upside down until I find them. I'll hunt here, there and everywhere. Because I cannot go anywhere without those keys, I will put fervent effort into that search. That's how we need to seek the kingdom of God. Proverbs 2:4 says it this way: We should seek for it as silver and hidden treasure. In other words, we search for the wisdom of God as we would for something valuable and precious. I have to have those keys! But even more important than anything in this life, I have to have the wisdom of God.

When you realize you are truly dependent on God for all of your needs—food on your table, clothes on your back, the job that you have, everything in your life—you go after Him and His ways with effort. You get passionate about your seeking. God becomes the primary thing in your life.

Ken and I both have been fervent seekers of God for years. When we first found out that if we sought God all other things would be added to us, we needed a lot of things! We were in a desperate situation. We were not just living at the bottom of the barrel. We were under the barrel trying to find a way out. We were broke, in debt, and seemingly without a financial future.

When we began to hear that God's Word is true and you can depend on it—that whatever He says, He will do—we began to seek and search His Word for answers.

We were so hungry for God, we couldn't get enough. We read every book and listened to every tape we could get our hands on about how to walk by faith. It was exciting!

When the Word of God was being preached in our area, we went to hear it—sometimes every night for days on end. Snow, ice, and rain didn't stop us. We found a way to get there so we could learn more of God's Word. We sought after the Lord with all our being, and as we did, we began to prosper.

Of course, that was many years ago, and today we are wonderfully blessed in every area of life. But we haven't forgotten where those blessings came from. We know that everything good we have—our family, our personal life, our marriage, and our material goods—came from seeking God and obeying Him. The more we seek Him, the more we love Him, and the more we love Him, the more we seek Him and the more we increase. It's a wonderful plan!

Jesus said, "Man shall not live by bread alone, but by every word that proceedeth out of the mouth of God" (Matt. 4:4). Ken and I know that's the truth. We have the life we live today because of hearing and doing God's Word. If we were to quit seeking Him, we would quit living. We are not about to quit seeking, that's for sure!

If you are in a desperate situation today, let me encourage you. It's not a bad thing to be desperate. Many people have come to God out of desperation. Many have turned to Him because they needed help in some area of their life, and they heard He could give it to them. That doesn't bother God. The reason His gospel is called the "good news" is because it lets people know that God cares about every area of their lives.

Initially, you may not come to Him for a spiritual reason. You may turn to Him because you are sick and need healing. You may be in financial difficulty or a seemingly hopeless marriage. You may seek Him because your children are without food and clothing. God takes those needs seriously. He wants to meet them and He can. He has the answer for every need in life!

Desperation will help you be fervent for a while. Then, as the crisis passes and God meets your needs, you won't seek God just because you need something from Him. You will start seeking Him because you love Him. As you grow and spend time in God's Word, you'll begin to find out how truly wonderful God is. Then you will seek Him because He is God, and because He is so good you want more of Him.

Your heart will go after Him and you will desire to build your life around Him and what He says. You will say as David did:

One thing have I asked of the Lord, that will I seek, inquire for, and [insistently] require: that I may dwell in the house of the Lord [in His presence] all the days of my life, to behold and gaze upon the beauty [the sweet attractiveness and the delightful loveliness] of the Lord and to meditate, consider, and inquire in His temple.... You have said, Seek My face [inquire for and require My presence as your vital need]. My heart says to You, Your face (Your presence), Lord, will I seek....

Psalm 27:4, 8 AMP

I have said those words to the Lord myself many times. I know that in order to turn from the ways of darkness to the ways of light, I cannot approach these things casually. I cannot go after the things of God just when it's convenient. I have to be diligent, I have to be fervent, and I have to be persistent. I have to be faithful.

But by the grace of God, I can do it. I can keep seeking God for the rest of my life and throughout eternity. I say to the Lord, "Your face will I seek!"

A Divine Safeguard

Some people might wonder why God structured His system of blessing this way. Why did He make seeking Him first the key that opens the door to His storehouse of blessings?

He did it because He is very wise and very loving. In an earlier chapter, we discussed the fact that material prosperity can be very harmful to people who are not prepared to handle it. People who have their priorities wrong or have no self-control can wreck their lives rapidly if they have enough money, because they can afford to indulge every natural passion of their flesh.

But godly prosperity has its own safeguard because you can only receive it by seeking God first. As you seek Him, your priorities get straightened out. By seeking Him you develop the fruit of the spirit—love, joy, peace, patience, gentleness, goodness, faithfulness, meekness, and self-control (Gal. 5:22). Once you develop those qualities, you won't be doing drugs. You won't be living in sexual immorality. You won't kill yourself early by wrongly using the money God gives you.

When you do what God says, riches will not be a danger to you.

You can have money without money having you. As you learn the ways of God, for example, you will find out that tithing is one of His principles of prosperity. He teaches His people to give the first 10 percent of their income to Him and His work on the earth. Tithing is a privilege.

Malachi 3:8–10 lets us know that the tithe belongs to God. So really it is not ours to keep. The Bible says if we keep the tithe, we are stealing from God! Although He does use this money to further His kingdom on the earth, it also helps us keep our priorities straight. It's a practical method we can use to put into action our desire to worship God and honor Him more than we honor material wealth. Money has force and power. If you don't do something to keep it in its place, it will eventually rule over you. Tithing helps us keep money in its proper place. Submitting to what God says in tithing and giving helps us to maintain a proper relationship with money. Obedience puts God first and refuses to put money first. Tithing brings God into our finances. It brings Him into partnership with us.

That is one reason tithing Christians are more blessed than Christians who do not tithe. God is freer to bless the tithers because they have put money in its proper place. He knows they will not let it ruin them. In other words, He knows they will not obey money, but will still obey Him even in prosperity. They have the inner strength and maturity to handle it properly.

When Ken and I first began to learn God's ways in the area of money, it was tough for a while. Not only did we find it was God's will for us to tithe and give offerings, we also saw a verse in the New Testament that said, "Keep out of debt and owe no man anything" (Rom. 13:8 AMP). Some people do not interpret that verse as literally as we did, and that's okay, but the way the Spirit of

God ministered that verse to us let us know that He did not want us ever to borrow money again.

Initially, it looked to us like obeying God in that area was going to be to our detriment. We did not have extra cash at the time. Everything we ever bought of any size had been purchased with debt. Even before I married him, Ken was in debt, so I married him and his "notes." (I think he must have borrowed money on his tricycle!)

We thought, *If we can't borrow money, how will we ever buy a car or furniture? How will we own a home? How will we conduct the finances of this ministry God has given us?*

Thank God, we decided to be obedient even though we could not see how it could work. We saw it in the Word so we determined to do it. We refused to go into debt even though at times it looked like that decision was going to ruin us.

Over the years, that decision has proven to be such a blessing. God has been so good and faithful to us. Both our personal finances and our ministry finances have exceeded anything we could have ever asked or dreamed back then. We have purchased vehicles, airplanes, houses, furnishings, the ministry headquarters, and the church building; ministered God's Word on radio and later on television six days a week; and preached around the world—all without borrowing money![13] Think of what we've saved in interest alone!

---

13. The one exception was many years ago when we were first learning how to live and conduct our business without debt. We took out a short-term loan to get out of a lease that was made out of the will of God. Of course, we did not realize that when we took the lease. The Lord permitted us to borrow the money to end the lease so we could sell the equipment. We sold it quickly with His help and paid the loan. We made a mistake, but God had mercy on us and delivered us. (I never said we did everything right!)

But one thing you need to know is this: Those finances did not come to us overnight. We just kept gradually increasing. As our spiritual capacity grew and our understanding of God grew, our blessings grew right alongside them at the same rate. As we learned to trust God more and obey Him more, He was able to give us and trust us with more.

Throughout our ministry, Ken and I have taught believers to have faith for prosperity—to believe in their hearts and confess with their mouths that God's will is to bless and increase them financially. We have taught them to abandon the poverty doctrines that are so contrary to the Word of God. We have taught God's Word that tells us God wants us to have every need met and that it is His good pleasure to prosper His servants.

Some people, however, have heard the message but still have not prospered. They say, "I'm willing to prosper. I believe God wants to bless me richly and I am confessing it every day! Why isn't it working?"

Because it takes more than just being willing to prosper. We must be willing to obey God in everything else as well. The road to prosperity is seeking God first and living in obedience to Him in every area of life. Only then can He safely prosper us as He desires to do. I don't think any of us have experienced all the prosperity God desires to give us. There is always increase in Him.

God's Way of Being Right

In the midst of my emphasis on obeying God and doing what He says to do, I want to make one thing perfectly clear. I am not saying in any way that we earn God's blessings by doing good works.

God is not measuring our performance to see if we "make the grade," then rewarding us with His blessings.

The truth is that God's wisdom is given to us. His Word is His wisdom. When His wisdom (the way He does things) is put into action, it brings blessing and increase. The result of obeying God's wisdom is prosperity in all areas of life.

Let's look again at Matthew 6:33 and read it in *The Amplified Bible,* which will give us additional insight. It says, "But seek (aim at and strive after) first of all His kingdom and His righteousness (His way of doing and being right), and then all these things taken together will be given you besides."

New Testament Christians do not earn right-standing with God by doing good things. We receive that right-standing as a gift from God by believing with our hearts and confessing with our mouths that Jesus has been raised from the dead and is our Lord (Rom. 10:9). Second Corinthians 5:21 says, "For he [God] hath made him [Jesus] to be sin for us, who knew no sin; that we might be made the righteousness of God in him."

When we put our faith in Jesus, the Bible says not only are we instantly given right-standing with God, but also something miraculous happens in our hearts. We become new creations. Second Corinthians 5:17 AMP says, "Therefore if any person is [ingrafted] in Christ (the Messiah) he is a new creation (a new creature altogether); the old [previous moral and spiritual condition] has passed away. Behold, the fresh and new has come!" We are, as Jesus said, "born again" (John 3:7). The Greek literally says "born from above." I like that. The old, sin nature that came to us through Adam is replaced by the nature of God. We are spiritually born of Him! We are made righteous—given right-standing.

Although we do not have to do good works to earn right-standing with God anymore, we suddenly want to do them because our heart has been re-created good. Hebrews 8:10–12 NIV describes it this way:

> This is the covenant I will make with the house of Israel after that time, declares the Lord. I will put my laws in their minds and write them on their hearts. I will be their God, and they will be my people. No longer will a man teach his neighbor, or a man his brother, saying, "Know the Lord," because they will all know me, from the least of them to the greatest. For I will forgive their wickedness and will remember their sins no more.

In the Old Testament, people obeyed God (or tried to obey Him) to be in right-standing with Him. Today we are not under law but grace. We obey God because we want to do it! Because we have been cleansed from sin and given God's own righteousness through the blood of Jesus, we have a heart to obey Him that will prevail over our natural desires, if we continue to seek God and give Him attention in our lives.

What's more, because Jesus freed us from the power of sin, and because the Father has sent His own Holy Spirit to dwell within us, we actually have the ability to live godly lives. We have the capacity not only to hear but to obey the voice of the Lord.

First Covenant people were not changed on the inside. Jesus had not yet come to set men free, so their nature was still of sin. They could be counted righteous if they obeyed the Law, but their hearts were constantly straying from God. Even when they tried to obey Him, they couldn't do it for very long because their fallen nature would drag them back into disobedience.

Throughout that era, because God loved people so, He longed for the day when that would change. He said as He watched the rebellious people of Israel, "Oh, that they had such a heart in them that they would fear Me and always keep all My commandments, that it might be well with them and with their children forever!" (Deut. 5:29 NKJV).

God looked forward to the day when, through the blood of Jesus, His people would have a new heart in them so they could obey Him and walk in His ways. Then He could bless them as richly as He desired. Thank God, we live in that day!

Taking the Narrow Way

We have seen that God's way of *being* right is to make Jesus our Savior and Lord. His way of *doing* right is for us to hear His Word and obey it.

The first place we hear God's Word is through the Bible. We need to read the Bible by faith, expecting the Spirit of God to speak revelation to us through it. We need to seek out what God says to us there about how we are to live our lives and then do what He says.

Hear and do. That's simple, isn't it? Yet over the years, I've discovered some people don't like that simple lifestyle. They want to complicate things by mixing what the Bible says with what they think or what other people think, then make up their own minds about what's right. They say that believing and obeying the Bible is too narrow-minded.

But the scriptural truth is, God's way is narrow! Jesus said:

> Enter by the narrow gate; for wide is the gate and broad is the way that leads to destruction, and there are many who go in by it. Because narrow is the gate and difficult is the way which leads to life, and there are few who find it.
>
> Matthew 7:13, 14 NKJV

From the very beginning, man has attempted to worship the things God created such as the earth, the things in the earth, and even himself. None of these things are God. God is the Creator of all. He is one God, not many. Consequently, there is only one way to Him, and that is His way. The world of human religion and ideas thinks and teaches that there are many doors through which one may have access to heaven. That is simply not true. The Bible teaches that Jesus is the only way to God. As one woman said, "Lots of people talk about God, but you've got to know His Boy!" The Scripture states in Ephesians 2:18, "For through him [Christ Jesus] we both have access by one Spirit unto the Father."

The Bible teaches that Jesus is the only way to God. The world teaches there are many ways. The Bible teaches there is only one God and He incorporates three persons—the Father, Son, and Holy Spirit. God is not the trees. He is not the earth. He is not the moon. He is not the universe. He is the Creator who made all those things.

The Bible teaches that whatever God says is right. It does not matter whether we think it is right or not. Nor does it matter how we feel about it. We do not get to vote on it. What God says in His written Word is right. It was right before we came on this earthly scene, and it will be right long after we are gone.

The world says, "If it feels good to you, it's right." But it doesn't matter how things feel to you. It matters what God says. You may or may not see things His way. Everyone in the whole world may say something different from what God says, but if they do, they'll all be wrong. Regardless of popular opinion, He is always right. It is His way or no way. His way is the only way.

Of course, people can ignore God's ways and come up with their own ways if they want, but in the end, they will be disappointed. They will end up sick, sorry, and sad. And if they make up their own way to get to heaven, they will end up in hell.

God's way is the only way that works. His way is the only way that is blessed, because His way is right.

If you think that's narrow-minded, you are correct. It's about as narrow as you can get.

Personally, I'm glad it's that way. It makes my life very simple. I don't have to be a rocket scientist to succeed. All I have to do is find out what God says and act on it. Then my way will be prosperous and I'll have good success (Josh. 1:8).

That's not just true for me; it's true for everyone. God's Word will work for anyone who will put it to work. The person who walks in the ways of God will prosper in everything he does. God's ways will make him a success!

As we seek to hear God's voice through His Word, we need to decide in advance that when He says something to us, we will agree with Him. We won't try to change Him and make Him agree with us. We will change and agree with Him. There may be times when we see something in God's Word that contradicts a belief we've held for many years. It may upset a mind-set we have had since childhood.

What do we do when that happens? We let that Word change our thinking. We let it renew our minds to think like God thinks and begin to walk in His will. As Romans 12:1–2 says:

I beseech you therefore, brethren, by the mercies of God, that ye present your bodies a living sacrifice, holy, acceptable unto God, which is your reasonable service. And be not conformed to this world: but be ye transformed by the renewing of your mind, that ye may prove what is that good, and acceptable, and perfect, will of God.

The more we let the Word of God change us, the more victory we are able to live in every day. I know that from experience. That is why I love the narrow way!

Drawing Near

As New Testament believers, we don't just read the Bible like a rule book and try to obey it. We have God's own Spirit living inside us. We know the Author of the Book! So we don't just read it; we draw near in our hearts to the One who wrote it and allow Him to speak to us. We seek Him until the words on the pages of our Bibles come alive in our hearts. We listen for His still, small voice inside us telling us just how to apply that Word to the situations in our lives.

You see, God does not want you just to have a relationship with paper and ink. He wants you to have a relationship with Him! "But isn't that the same thing?" you ask. "If I know what the Bible says, don't I know Him?"

Not necessarily. The Pharisees proved that. In one confrontation, Jesus said to them, "You search the Scriptures, for in them you think you have eternal life; and these are they which testify of Me. But you are not willing to come to Me that you may have life" (John 5:39, 40 NKJV).

For the Word of God to truly give us life, we must draw near to the person of God. We must come to Him in fellowship and obedience.

Some believers are reluctant to do that because they are not sure God will reveal Himself to them. They think, *What if I spend time seeking God and nothing happens? What if I don't sense His presence or discern His voice? I will have wasted my time.*

If that's your concern, let me put it to rest right now. According to the Bible, it's impossible for you to seek God and go unrewarded. It's impossible for you to come near to Him with your heart and find Him standing at a distance from you. The Bible is very clear about that. Again and again, it gives us such assurances as:

Draw nigh to God, and he will draw nigh to you (James 4:8).

Ask, and it shall be given you; seek, and ye shall find; knock, and it shall be opened unto you: For every one that asketh receiveth; and he that seeketh findeth; and to him that knocketh it shall be opened (Matt. 7:7, 8).

The young lions do lack, and suffer hunger: but they that seek the Lord shall not want any good thing (Ps. 34:10).

But without faith it is impossible to please him: for he that cometh to God must believe that he is, and that he is a rewarder of them that diligently seek Him (Heb. 11:6).

God Will Reward You

In Hebrews 11:6, we see that it takes faith to draw near to God. You cannot draw near to God in unbelief. You cannot draw near thinking doubtful thoughts like, *This probably isn't going to do any good. God won't speak to me.* You will not get anywhere that way.

In coming to God, we must be confident, believing not only that He exists, but that He is the rewarder. We must trust in the fact that He will reward us with His manifest presence if we will earnestly and diligently seek Him.

One thing that will build your faith and confidence is the realization that God wants to fellowship with you far more than you want to fellowship with Him. He isn't trying to hide Himself from you. He is not playing "hard to get."

He sought us long before we ever began seeking Him. Look back through the Bible and you can see that God has been seeking to have fellowship with mankind, to speak to them and meet with them, from the very beginning. In the Garden of Eden, God came to walk with Adam and Eve in the cool of the day. Even after they disobeyed and hid from Him, He came looking for them. He called out to Adam, "Where are you?" (Gen. 3:9 AMP).

Then again, we see in Exodus 19 when the Lord brought the Israelites out of Egypt, He desired to meet and talk with them at Mount Sinai: "And the Lord said unto Moses, Lo, I come unto thee in a thick cloud, that the people may hear when I speak with thee, and believe thee for ever. And Moses told the words of the people unto the Lord" (v. 9).

If you read that passage, you will see that God instructed Moses to set up boundaries around the mountain so that when He drew near to speak to the people, they would not rush toward Him to get too close. (They were not born-again people. They were spiritually dead. Such close proximity to the Lord would have literally killed them.) God wanted to come as near to them as He could without hurting them.

> And all the people saw the thunderings, and the lightnings, and the noise of the trumpet, and the mountain smoking: and when the people saw it, they removed, and stood afar off. And they said unto Moses, Speak thou with us, and we will hear: but let not God speak with us, lest we die.
>
> Exodus 20:18, 19

God's idea was to come down to the people and let them hear His voice so they would do what He said. He wanted to draw near and speak to them. But they did not go for it. They did not draw near. They were afraid and trembled. They drew back.

Of course, what really made the Israelites withdraw from fellowship with God at that time was the sin factor. In the presence of His righteousness, holiness, and power, they were afraid and ashamed because they were unredeemed people still enslaved by sin. They were unworthy to stand in God's presence and they knew it.

Thank God, the blood of Jesus has taken care of that for us today. When He died for our sins, He drew us to God by making a way for us to be forgiven and cleansed. He made it possible for us to stand in the presence of our holy God without a sense of guilt or shame. When God provided the sacrifice of Jesus for us, He drew near to us in the most powerful way possible, and He made the way for us to draw near to Him.

We can be confident God will meet us in our times of prayer when we realize that the whole reason Jesus came was "to seek and to save that which was lost" (Luke 19:10). His purpose was to restore the lost fellowship between God and mankind, drawing us once again into personal fellowship with Him. As He said, "If I be lifted up from the earth, [I] will draw all men unto me" (John 12:32).

The New Testament echoes that truth again and again.

As we respond to God by seeking Him in return, we will discover we don't have to go very far to find Him. He's right here with us and in us. As Ephesians 2:13–14 says, "But now in Christ Jesus ye who sometimes were far off are made nigh by the blood of Christ. For he is our peace...."

We do not have to search far and wide to find our heavenly Father because we have already been brought near to Him by the blood of Jesus!

So we can do what Hebrews 10:19–22 says:

> Having therefore, brethren, boldness to enter into the holiest by the blood of Jesus, by a new and living way, which he hath consecrated for us, through the veil, that is to say, his flesh; and having an high priest over the house of God; let us draw near with a true heart in full assurance of faith....

We are not like those people who cowered at Mount Sinai. We can rush right into the throne room of God. Through Jesus, we have been made righteous so we can freely fellowship with Him.

"But Gloria," you may say, "I don't feel like I can draw near to God because I've been sinning and I know it."

If that's the case, then repent and let the blood of Jesus cleanse you afresh and anew. "If we confess our sins, he [God] is faithful and just to forgive us our sins, and to cleanse us from all unrighteousness....My little children, these things write I unto you, that ye sin not. And if any man sin, we have an advocate with the Father, Jesus Christ the righteous" (1 John 1:9; 2:1). So if you know you have been doing wrong or you have failed to obey Him in some area, repent of it and get it straight. Be quick to repent when you miss God. Come boldly before God's throne and receive mercy and forgiveness for those sins, and then let Him give you the grace and power to walk free of them (Heb. 4:16).

Once you do that, you can be confident that God will speak to you by His Spirit. He will draw near to you as you draw near to Him.

Remember this: God isn't holding out on you. He's always trying to get blessing to you, and the greatest blessing He can give you is the fellowship of His own Spirit. Everyone who asks for that receives it. Everyone who seeks it, finds it.

I have heard one testimony after another of people who were not even born again, people who were right in the middle of the most sinful lifestyle imaginable—yet they cried out to God and said, "Lord, if You're really there, reveal Yourself to me!"

I have heard wonderful stories of how God moved on people like that, letting them know He was not only present with them... He loved them.

How much more can we expect Him to speak to us, His very own children, who are seeking to live lives that are pleasing to Him? How much more can we be confident that He will, indeed, draw near to us!

CHAPTER 8

Looking for a Receiver

For the eyes of the Lord run to and fro throughout the
whole earth, to show himself strong in the behalf of them
whose heart is perfect toward him.

2 CHRONICLES 16:9

In all the reading I've done as I've researched the goodness of God, the quote I keep coming back to is the one cited by Jewish scholar David Baron. Except for quotes from the Bible itself, I believe his words best summarize God's unlimited ability and desire to bless His people. Although I included his comments in an earlier chapter, they have had such impact on me, I want to quote them again:

> Goodness is that attribute of God whereby He loveth to communicate to all who can or will receive it, all good... Himself, who is the fulness and universality of good, Creator of all good, not in one way, not in one kind of goodness only, but absolutely, without beginning, without limit, without measure, save that whereby without measurement He possesseth and embraceth all excellence, all perfection, all blessedness, all good.

This good His goodness bestoweth on all and each, according to the capacity of each to receive it; nor is there any limit to His giving, save His creatures' capacity of receiving, which also is a good gift from Him.

Again and again, the Scriptures teach us that God is unlimited in His resources and His abilities. He has placed enough riches in this earth to take care of everyone who will turn to Him. We do not have to worry about God's ability to take care of our needs. Our only concern is to develop our capacity to receive. We have to spiritually be in position by hearing and obeying God's Word. Ephesians 3:20 reminds us God is able to do exceeding abundantly above all that we ask or think, according to the power, the capacity, that works in us. What we have to do is receive what God offers.

A few years ago when I was watching the Super Bowl, the Lord used one particular play in that game to graphically illustrate that truth. Usually I'm not much of a football fan. The only reason I was interested in the game that day was because St. Louis was playing. Two of their key players, quarterback Kurt Warner and wide receiver Isaac Bruce, are strong believers and I wanted to see them. I wanted to help!

At a critical point in the game, I was watching Kurt Warner when he drew back to throw a pass. As he looked down the field, what was he looking for? A receiver! Isaac Bruce was in position, ready and able to receive. He threw the ball. The pass was completed and they won the Super Bowl! It was a marvelous play.

Since then, I've thought about that moment again and again. God has used it to illustrate that He is always looking for a receiver, just like Kurt Warner was that day. God has in His hand blessings beyond human comprehension. He is longing to pass them to His family. He has spiritual victories He wants us to win. He has rewards and trophies He wants us to enjoy.

But He cannot do it unless He can find someone to receive! God has to have a receiver!

Of course, I did not just learn that from a football game. I learned it from the Bible. Second Chronicles 16:9 says, "For the eyes of the Lord run to and fro throughout the whole earth, to show himself strong in the behalf of them whose heart is perfect toward him...." The word translated *perfect* there actually means "devoted, faithful, dedicated, loyal and consecrated." This verse tells us that God is constantly searching for that one whose heart is devoted to Him so that He might demonstrate His kindness and power in his or her life. He is continually looking for a receiver.

One thing for sure, Isaac Bruce was ready to receive! He was waiting with outstretched arms. He was in position. He was intently watching the quarterback. He was not looking at the crowd wondering whether or not his mother was watching. He had his eye on the ball.

He was not standing with his hands clasped behind his back thinking, *I'll be glad when this is over.*

He was not thinking, *When do we get to eat?*

No! No! Isaac was into what he was doing—spirit, soul, and body. He was ready and available. He was focused!

Notice that verse does not say God is looking for someone who is outwardly perfect. He is not looking for someone who never makes a mistake. He is looking for a devoted heart. God is a heart-searcher. The Bible says, "Man looketh on the outward appearance, but the Lord looketh on the heart" (1 Sam. 16:7). He is looking for people who love Him and will wholeheartedly obey Him. As Jesus said, "If a man love me, he will keep my words: and my Father will love him, and we will come unto him, and make our abode with him" (John 14:23).

God doesn't care what race, gender, or nationality you are. He is not inspecting how perfectly you dress or keep house or pursue your career. He does not check externals. He is looking for a heart that is turned toward Him in love and faith. Jeremiah 17:10 says, "I the Lord search the heart, I try the reins...." The word *reins* means "thoughts and affections." He doesn't just listen to what we say when we are in church. He looks to see what's in our hearts.

God will pass by a thousand people to get to one person who has a heart to love, obey, and believe Him. I appreciate that about Him. He does not just deal with people in masses. He is so important and powerful that He could just deal with nations if He wanted. Even so, He chooses not only to deal with nations, but to deal personally with every individual inside those nations!

He will pick one person out of a million who will give his heart to Him if that is all He can find, and He will show Himself strong on behalf of that one. He will find one person who, because of his heart condition, has the capacity to receive, and He will pour out His blessings upon him. You can be that one!

God is good and wants to do good! He wants to do miracles and bless His family with such bountiful gifts from heaven that it astounds the world. That is just the way God is. He is always look- ing for a receiver. If you live in the darkest part of Africa and you seek God with your heart, He will find you and answer your call.

Find Out What the Bible Says

One passage of Scripture that addresses the issue of receiving is the parable of the sower. In Mark 4, Jesus speaks of four different kinds of ground, each representing certain groups of people. Every group heard the Word of God, but only one group enjoyed the fruit of it in their lives.

The first group was likened to hard, uncultivated ground by the wayside. They heard the Word of God but did not let it in their heart in such a way that it could take root and grow. The second group Jesus compared to stony ground. They heard the Word and received it in a very shallow way. As a result, when persecution and circumstantial pressure came, they were offended and let go of the Word they had heard. The third group was likened to thorny ground. Their hearts were so overcrowded with worldly desires and worries that the Word they heard was choked and became unfruitful.

The final group, the good-ground group, was different. They not only heard the Word but *received* it and did not let it go. They *received* it. They took it. They embraced it and held on to it. They refused to let worldly pleasures and cares or unbelief crowd it out of their hearts.

If we want to enjoy the fruit of God's Word in our lives and have the fullness of His goodness manifest to us, we have to be good receivers. Let's take a closer look at the concept of receiving. We do not want to fumble the ball after we receive it.

According to Webster's dictionary, the word *receive* means "to come into possession of or acquire; to assimilate through the mind or senses; to permit to enter in, to welcome or to greet; to accept as authoritative, true and accurate; to take from the weight of something as an impression or mark."

We can apply each of those definitions and learn something about how we need to respond when we hear or read the Word of God.

To be good receivers of God's Word, first we must "come into possession of or acquire it." In other words, we must put forth the effort it takes to find out what God has said.

In this day, especially in the United States of America, there is no excuse for anyone to be ignorant about the Bible. There is a myriad of translations available in bookstores—many written so simply that anyone can understand them. Many Christian outreach ministries give Bibles free of charge to those who cannot afford to buy them. There are good churches that teach the Word in every area of the country. Christian television broadcasts can be seen almost anywhere these days. Christian radio broadcasts cover the earth. Great meetings are conducted around the world. Bible-based books and teaching tapes and CDs abound.

The Internet is a tremendous resource available around the world. Kenneth Copeland Ministries even broadcasts our meetings live as well as the daily and Sunday television programs on the Internet. (You can find us at www.kcm.org.) Check it out. There is so much teaching of God's Word available to you absolutely free!

The first step to being a good receiver is to take advantage of these resources. Don't just sit around wishing you knew what the Bible says. Take action. Jesus said to believe you receive when you pray (Mark 11:24). Receiving requires action and puts faith in motion. *Receive* in Mark 11:24 in Greek means "to take"! You have to take hold of whatever you desire when you pray and retain it until it is manifest.

As the definition of receive says, "assimilate [the Scriptures] through your mind and your senses." Start reading, studying, listening, and learning what God is saying to you. Get the Word of God in your heart until it talks to you from the inside day and night. Then every time you encounter a new challenge in life, the Word of God will show you what to do. When temptation, test, and trial come to you, the Word will come up into your thoughts. That Word will give you direction and bring victory if you obey it. John 15:7 says, "If ye abide in me, and my words abide in you, ye shall ask what ye will, and it shall be done unto you."

Let God's Word change you and correct you.

Many Christians live in defeat even after making Jesus Lord of their lives, because they keep living the same old way as if nothing happened. They keep living as though they have no covenant blessing from God. They do not know what the Bible says about their covenant, so they cannot believe it and act on it. If they don't know, how can they believe it? How can they believe what they have not yet heard? Romans 10:14, 16–17 says:

How then shall they call on him in whom they have not believed? and how shall they believe in him of whom they have not heard? and how shall they hear without a preacher?...But they have not all obeyed the gospel. For Esaias saith, Lord, who hath believed our report? So then faith cometh by hearing, and hearing by the word of God.

They have been born again in the Name of Jesus—all the blessings of God are theirs, but because they have not assimilated the

Word of God by keeping it before their eyes and in their ears to get it into their heart, they have not developed their capacity to receive those blessings. Faith comes only by hearing and believing the Word of God.

That is why every Christian should heed the instructions in Proverbs 4:20–23:

> My son, attend to my words; incline thine ear unto my sayings. Let them not depart from thine eyes; keep them in the midst of thine heart. For they are life unto those that find them, and health to all their flesh. Keep thy heart with all diligence; for out of it are the issues of life.

I will warn you right now, the devil will pressure you to do just the opposite of what these verses tell you to do. He knows you will become a strong receiver if you keep God's Word in your eyes and ears, so he will try to influence you to watch trash on television instead of read your Bible. He will try to talk you into listening to music or watching movies where people take the Name of the Lord in vain and show no reverence toward God. He will push you to check out pornographic sites on the Internet so he can get a stronghold in your life.

Get a grip on this truth: "The eye is the lamp of the body. So if your eye is sound, your entire body will be full of light. But if your eye is unsound, your whole body will be full of darkness. If then the very light in you is darkened, how dense is that darkness! No one can serve two masters..." (Matt. 6:22–24 AMP).

Light or darkness—good or evil—enters into your heart

through your eyes! Look again at the parable of the sower: "And the cares of this world, and the deceitfulness of riches, and the lusts of other things entering in, choke the word, and it becometh unfruitful" (Mark 4:19).

Jesus said if you don't understand this parable, how can you understand any? Things that are in your heart today have come through your eyes and your ears. They are the gates to your heart. Jesus said in Mark 4:24 AMP, "Be careful what you are hearing." Proverbs 6:23 tells us, "For the commandment is a lamp; and the law is light; and reproofs of instruction are the way of life."

Proverbs 23:7 says, "As [a man] thinketh in his heart, so is he." That is why the Apostle Paul instructed believers, "Brethren, whatever is true, whatever is worthy of reverence and is honorable and seemly, whatever is just, whatever is pure, whatever is lovely and lovable, whatever is kind and winsome and gracious, if there is any virtue and excellence, if there is anything worthy of praise, think on and weigh and take account of these things [fix your minds on them]" (Phil. 4:8 AMP).

The Jews teach that there are seven gates to the heart as there were seven gates to the Temple. They are two eyes, two ears, two nostrils, and one mouth. These gates are the gates to your temple. They are to be guarded with your life! "Keep your heart with all diligence; for out of it are the issues of life" (Prov. 4:23).

Out of your heart comes forth the God-kind of life! So, to live a victorious life, you must guard your heart—guard your heart gates and you guard your life.

The devil knows this works. He knows that if you fill your heart with the things of the world, those things will choke the Word so it will not have any effect on your life. He also knows that if you let the Word of God in your eyes, ears, and heart, it will take over your mouth, your desires, and your life and choke him!

So what are you to do?

Give the devil no place in your life. I did not say give him just a little place. The Bible says give him no place: "Neither give place to the devil" (Eph. 4:27). Zero. Naught.

Psalm 101:3 says, "I will set *no* wicked thing before mine eyes...." Jesus said, "Be careful what you are hearing" (Mark 4:24 AMP). Don't give the devil your eyes and ears. Give them to God. Keep them occupied with Him and His Word.

Someone might say, "I've been doing that for years!" Then keep doing it.

I don't care how long we have been walking with the Lord, we have to continue keeping His Word in our eyes and in our ears so that it stays in the midst of our hearts. We cannot live on last year's Word, or even last week's Word. We have to have the Word of God working in us today in order to keep our thinking sound and our words straight.

One reason this is so necessary is because we are surrounded by unbelievers and a world full of people who are trying to go to hell as fast as they can. We live in a world that ridicules and shuns God and does not give Him any reverence. Worldly people do not care what God says about a situation—they are going to do what they want. That downward flow is continually pulling on us. For us to counter it and stay with the flow of God, we have to be continually receiving His Word into our hearts through our eyes and ears. It is well worth the effort in order to live in life and health!

Patience Is a Vital Part

Looking again at Webster's definition, we find another key to being a good receiver. As you discover what the Word says, permit it to enter your heart. Welcome it. Receive it like a gift from God. Let it make an impression or mark on your life. Let it change how you think and how you live.

Remember this: Every time you make a choice to receive and obey God's Word, you increase your spiritual capacity another notch. Every time you reject God's Word or refuse to act on it, your spiritual capacity decreases.

Do not let natural, human reasoning or religious tradition cause you to resist the truth you see in God's Word and to erect barriers against it. For example, when you read in Matthew 6:33 where God says He will add everything else to you if you will just seek His kingdom first, do not say, "Well, I don't know about that. I heard about one preacher who put God first and he didn't make it."

No, determine beforehand that you are going to believe and welcome God's Word more than anybody else's opinions, word, or testimony. Decide in advance that if anybody's experience, including your own, seems to contradict the Word of God, you are going to throw out the experience and keep the Word. As Romans 3:4 says, "Let God be true, but every man a liar."

If you will take that attitude and continue to welcome God's Word into your heart and meditate on it, you will grow strong in faith. You will become so assured that the Word is true, no one will be able to convince you otherwise. Somebody might try to tell you that God is not good and He is not going to meet your needs. People may try to talk you out of your confidence in Him, but they won't be able to do it. That is faith.

As Hebrews 1:11 NASB says, "Faith is the assurance of things hoped for, the conviction of things not seen." Once you have heard the Word of God and mixed it with faith, you are absolutely assured in your heart that God is going to do what He says. You have such strong conviction He is going to be good to you in every situation that even if you cannot see that goodness yet, you know in your heart it's yours. Hebrews 11:1 AMP says it this way, "Faith [perceives] as real fact what is not revealed to the senses."

When you have faith in God's goodness, even if something bad happens you'll expect God to turn it around for good. For instance, if you were to lose your job, the first thing you should think is, *God has a better job for me now! He wants to promote me!* If you are loving and obeying Him, that's the right way to think because He always has a promotion for you. He always wants to increase you.

A few years ago, one of the Partners of this ministry had exactly that experience. He'd had an important, lucrative position with his company but something happened and he lost that job. About that time, he came across Ken's book *The Laws of Prosperity* and found out that God is good and that God wanted him to be financially blessed. So he took that book and his Bible and went to a fast-food restaurant every day to study because he didn't have anywhere else to go. He would sit there, drink coffee, and build his faith by studying and meditating on the Word of God.

Not only did that man prosper, he prospered so greatly that he became the first person ever to give a million dollars to help with the work of this ministry. When trouble came his way, he turned his heart, his eyes, and his ears to God. He became a receiver, and as a result, he is a very wealthy man today and still increasing.

When your faith perceives as fact what is not yet revealed to your senses, you can be patient through the tough times for God's goodness to be revealed. That's important because patience is a vital part of receiving. As Luke's account of the parable of the sower says, the heart that is good ground brings forth fruit "with patience" (Luke 8:15).

If we're going to be good receivers, we cannot give up and stop believing God's Word when circumstances put us under pressure. When we get an evil report and we're told our illness has no cure, or we're about to go bankrupt, we have to continue to believe we receive. We have to be steadfast in the hard places when to the natural eye, it looks like we are not going to make it. We cannot quit. We must hold fast to that which is good. First Thessalonians 5:20–21 says, "Despise not prophesyings. Prove all things; hold fast that which is good."

People who are enjoying the blessings of God today have had many opportunities to get discouraged in the past. They have experienced hard times. They have felt pressure. But they kept believing God anyway. They just continued trusting God and expecting to see His goodness manifest in their lives.

Someone might say, "Well, I don't know why we have to do that."

We have to do it because we are believers! We should not be shocked that we have to trust God and have faith through difficult times. We should not let that scare us. After all, believing God is what we do! We are overcomers, and overcoming is what we do.

God has given us all the equipment necessary to believe. He has given us a reborn spirit in the image of Himself. He has given us His faith and love in our hearts. He has given us the fruit of the spirit which includes patience to help us stay strong until the answer comes. We have the wisdom of God available to us at all times just for the asking. We have Jesus Christ Himself at the right hand of the Father ever praying and interceding for us. We have a Father who loves us and is good all the time.

We have everything we need to walk by faith. It just takes some effort. We have to press in and refuse to quit. It takes time in some cases to see God's goodness become a reality in the midst of dark circumstances, but if we do not quit we will see God come shining through. This has been our experience for more than forty years!

Four Good Receivers

One of the best ways to increase our capacity to receive from God is to study the accounts the Bible gives of people who were good receivers. There are many, many such people, and there is something we can learn from all of them. I want to focus on four of my favorites: the woman with the issue of blood; Jairus, the synagogue ruler; the Roman centurion; and the beggar, blind Bartimaeus.

We find the first two in Mark 5. Their stories are so intertwined in Scripture that they are best told together:

> Behold, there cometh one of the rulers of the synagogue, Jairus by name; and when he saw [Jesus], he fell at his feet, and besought him greatly, saying, My little daughter lieth at the point of death: I pray thee, come and lay thy hands on her, that she may be healed; and she shall live. And Jesus went

with him; and much people followed him, and thronged him. And a certain woman, which had an issue of blood twelve years, and had suffered many things of many physicians, and had spent all that she had, and was nothing bettered, but rather grew worse, when she had heard of Jesus, came in the press behind, and touched his garment. For she said, If I may touch but his clothes, I shall be whole. And straightway the fountain of her blood was dried up; and she felt in her body that she was healed of that plague. And Jesus, immediately knowing in himself that virtue had gone out of him, turned him about in the press, and said, Who touched my clothes? And his disciples said unto him, Thou seest the multitude thronging thee, and sayest thou, Who touched me? And he looked round about to see her that had done this thing. But the woman fearing and trembling, knowing what was done in her, came and fell down before him, and told him all the truth. And he said unto her, Daughter, thy faith hath made thee whole; go in peace, and be whole of thy plague.

Mark 5:22–34

Let's look first at the woman with the issue of blood. She was facing some very bad circumstances. She was not only sick, she was sick and broke. She could have easily stayed in her room and felt sorry for herself. She could have sat on her bed, crying and thinking, *If God is good, why has He let this happen to me?*

But something happened to her that made her decide not to do that. What was it? She heard and welcomed to her heart the Word about Jesus. She had no doubt heard that He was healing people and she believed it.

What's more, she acted on her faith. The first action she took was to open her mouth and say what she believed. Notice, she did not say what she felt or how terrible her life had been. She spoke words of faith, saying, "If I may touch but his clothes, I shall be whole" (Mark 5:28). According to *The Amplified Bible,* she did not just say that once, either. She repeated it again and again. She "kept saying" it.

Then she took the next step of faith. She left her home, in spite of the fact that it was against the Jewish law for her to be in public in her condition. She fought and pushed her way through the crowd that was surrounding Jesus. She reached out to touch His clothes.

Sure enough, exactly what she said happened. She was instantly healed. Other people were touching Jesus, but theirs was not the touch of faith so they were not receiving anything from Him. She was the one who was believing, speaking, and acting on the Word she had heard about Him, so she is the one who received! According to Jesus, it was her faith (her believing and saying) that made her whole. Jesus said, "Daughter, thy faith hath made thee whole; go in peace, and be whole of thy plague" (v. 34).

Wholehearted Faith with Words to Match

Look at how Jairus, the synagogue ruler, received. We can immediately see striking similarities between his behavior and that of the woman with the issue of blood. He, too, had obviously heard the reports of Jesus' love and power and had believed them.

We also find him speaking words of faith. After telling Jesus about his sick daughter, he said, "Come and lay Your hands on her, that she may be healed, and she will live" (Mark 5:23 NKJV). Pay special attention to those last three words. They are not a request; they are a declaration of faith: "She will live."

Watch Jesus' response to Jairus, and you will see a clear picture of how God always responds to those who reach out to Him in faith, trusting His goodness and power. Jesus did not say, "Listen here, Jairus, who do you think you are to tell Me what to do? Maybe I don't want to come to your house. I'm the Son of God and you're not. Who are you to tell Me to lay My hands on somebody for healing? Maybe I want to do it some other way."

No, Jesus did not say any of those things. On the contrary, He immediately turned and went with Jairus, intending to do exactly what Jairus said in faith. Jesus was easily entreated. He was easy to receive from.

Although the Bible does not specifically say so, I believe Jairus had to exercise great patience to receive his miracle. He had already told Jesus his daughter was at the point of death. Time was of the essence. But in spite of the critical nature of the situation, Jesus allowed an interruption. He stopped, spoke to the woman who had been healed of the issue of blood, listened to her tell the story of her illness, and confirmed to her that her faith had made her whole.

I can just imagine how Jairus must have felt. Surely he was thinking, *Hurry up, Jesus! We don't have much time! Can't You talk to this woman later?*

To make matters worse—much worse—by the time that incident was over, Jairus had received very bad news:

> While he [Jesus] yet spake [with the woman], there came from the ruler of the synagogue's house certain which said,

Thy daughter is dead: why troublest thou the Master any further? As soon as Jesus heard the word that was spoken, he saith unto the ruler of the synagogue, Be not afraid, only believe.... And he cometh to the house of the ruler of the synagogue, and seeth the tumult, and them that wept and wailed greatly. And when he was come in, he saith unto them, Why make ye this ado, and weep? the damsel is not dead, but sleepeth. And they laughed him to scorn. But when he had put them all out, he taketh the father and the mother of the damsel, and them that were with him, and entereth in where the damsel was lying. And he took the damsel by the hand, and said unto her, Talitha cumi; which is, being interpreted, Damsel, I say unto thee, arise. And straightway the damsel arose, and walked; for she was of the age of twelve years. And they were astonished with a great astonishment.

Mark 5:35–42

I think it is very interesting that when Jairus received news of his daughter's death, Jesus immediately said to him, "Be not afraid, only believe!" Why was Jesus so quick and definite about that? He knew Jairus's wholehearted faith and his faith-filled words had put him in position to receive his daughter's healing. He did not want Jairus to step out of position by allowing fear to get in his heart and choke his faith. Jesus did not want Jairus to diminish his capacity to receive by speaking words of doubt and fear.

Thankfully, Jairus did exactly what Jesus said. As a result, Jesus did exactly what Jairus had said. He went to his house, took the girl by the hand, and told her to rise. She came back to life healed just like Jairus said she would!

Jesus Changes His Plans

Some people seem to have the idea that faith offends God. Or maybe they have the idea that God doesn't want to be bothered. Religious people especially seem to get upset at the idea that anyone would be bold enough to expect God to do exactly what they asked Him to do. But the fact is, faith does not offend God; it pleases Him. In fact, Hebrews 11:6 says just the opposite: "But without faith it is impossible to please him: for he that cometh to God must believe that he is, and that he is a rewarder of them that diligently seek him."

God isn't bothered by the boldness of the one who comes to Him in faith, because that boldness isn't inspired by the person's confidence in himself. It's inspired by his confidence in God—in His goodness, His love, and His power.

One of the best examples of such confidence can be found in Matthew 8, in the story of the Roman centurion:

When Jesus was entered into Capernaum, there came unto him a centurion, beseeching him, and saying, Lord, my servant lieth at home sick of the palsy, grievously tormented. And Jesus saith unto him, I will come and heal him. The centurion answered and said, Lord, I am not worthy that thou shouldest come under my roof: but speak the word only, and my servant shall be healed. For I am a man under authority, having soldiers under me: and I say to this man, Go, and he goeth; and to another, Come, and he cometh; and to my servant, Do this, and he doeth it. When Jesus heard it, he marvelled, and said to them that followed, Verily I say unto you, I have not found so great faith, no, not in Israel.... And Jesus said unto the centurion, Go thy way; and as thou hast believed, so be it done unto thee. And his servant was healed in the selfsame hour.

vv. 5–13

Isn't that amazing? Not only did Jesus do what this man asked Him to do, He changed his plans in accordance with the man's next request. Jesus intended to go to his house and heal the servant, but the centurion said, in essence, "No, I'd rather You not come to my house because I'm not worthy. Just speak the Word and my servant will be healed."

Once again, notice the centurion put himself in position to receive just as Jairus and the woman with the issue of blood had done. He heard and believed the Word about Jesus. He spoke words of faith, saying, "My servant will be healed." And he put action to his faith by coming to the Lord.

Making the Faith Connection

Our final example of good receiving is found in the healing of blind Bartimaeus. Mark 10:46–52 tells us the story:

As he [Jesus] went out of Jericho with his disciples and a great number of people, blind Bartimaeus, the son of Timaeus, sat by the highway side begging. And when he heard that it was Jesus of Nazareth, he began to cry out, and say, Jesus, thou son of David, have mercy on me. And many charged him that he should hold his peace: but he cried the more a great deal, Thou son of David, have mercy on me. And Jesus stood still, and commanded him to be called. And they call the blind man, saying unto him, Be of good comfort, rise; he calleth thee. And he, casting away his garment, rose, and came to Jesus. And Jesus answered and said unto him, What wilt thou that I should do unto thee? The blind man said unto him, Lord, that I might receive my sight. And Jesus said unto him, Go thy way; thy faith hath made thee whole. And immediately he received his sight, and followed Jesus in the way.

One of my favorite things about Bartimaeus is that he refused to let the people around him discourage him. They did not have the faith in God's goodness that he had. They had such limited understanding of God's love that they thought Jesus would not be interested in a seemingly worthless, blind beggar. But Bartimaeus had heard about Jesus. No doubt he had heard of His mercy and kindness and His healing power. And he believed.

So when the people tried to shut him up, he cried out all the louder, "Jesus, thou son of David, have mercy on me!" Why did he cry so loudly? Because he was convinced in his heart that if Jesus heard him, He would answer. Jesus would deliver Him and he knew it. This was his chance of a lifetime.

Jesus heard him and when He did, He stood still and commanded that Bartimaeus be called. Aggressive faith always gets Jesus' attention. Of course, then all the religious people changed their tune. They stopped telling him to be quiet and said, "Be of good comfort. Jesus is calling for you!"

What Bartimaeus did next was one of the most beautiful expressions of faith recorded in the New Testament. He threw off his cloak. History reveals that action had special significance. One commentary tells us, "The 'cloak' (Mark 10:50) is an outer garment, used as a coat in cold weather and as bedding at night, and might have been spread before him for use in his daytime begging if he had no pouch. The act of casting it aside may signify his forsaking dependence on anything else and trusting only in Jesus."[14]

I firmly believe that when Bartimaeus threw off his cloak, he was never planning to use it as a begging pouch again. By that act, he was making a very clear statement. He was saying, "I'm not a blind man anymore. Jesus has heard me, and I'm as good as healed!"

Notice what Jesus asked Bartimaeus next. He said, "What do you want Me to do for you?" (v. 51 AMP).

Bartimaeus knew the answer to that question. He said boldly, "Master, let me receive my sight" (v. 51).

Bartimaeus was in perfect position to receive. God was looking to and fro throughout the whole earth for someone to whom He could show Himself strong...and He found Bartimaeus full of faith in Jesus, speaking and acting with great confidence in His goodness and His power. The connection was made and Jesus said, "Go your way; your faith has healed you" (v. 52 AMP).

I want you to be impressed by Jesus' goodness and how willing He was to express that goodness. Whatever those who came to Him for help said, He said. Jesus acted on *their* words! He, being just like the Father, was easy to receive from.

The woman with the issue of blood said, "If I only touch His garments, I shall be restored to health" (Mark 5:28 AMP). The moment she touched it, she received her healing. Jesus accommodated her.

---

14. C. S. Keener, *The IVP Bible, background commentary: New Testament* (Mark 10:49, 11:1). (Downers Grove, Ill.: InterVarsity Press, 1993).

Whatever the centurion asked, Jesus was willing to do, so that his desire could be answered and the servant healed.

Jesus asked Bartimaeus, "What can I do for you?" Bartimaeus told Him what he wanted. Jesus said, "Your faith has made you whole." What Bartimaeus said, Jesus did. He immediately received his sight and followed Jesus.

Look again at Acts 10:38: "How God anointed Jesus of Nazareth with the Holy Ghost and with power: who went about doing good, and healing all that were oppressed of the devil; for God was with him." Jesus was so good that He went about doing good and healing all who would receive.

When you've seen Jesus, you've seen the Father:

Philip saith unto him, Lord, show us the Father, and it sufficeth us. Jesus saith unto him, Have I been so long time with you, and yet hast thou not known me, Philip? he that hath seen me hath seen the Father; and how sayest thou then, Show us the Father? Believest thou not that I am in the Father, and the Father in me? the words that I speak unto you I speak not of myself: but the Father that dwelleth in me, he doeth the works.

John 14:8–10

The Bible says, "Every good gift and every perfect gift is from above, and cometh down from the Father of lights, with whom is no variableness, neither shadow of turning" (James 1:17). There is no changing in Him.

Hebrews 13:8 says, "Jesus Christ the same yesterday, and today, and for ever." Jesus and the Father are still going about doing good and healing all who will receive.[15] "The Lord is good to all: and his tender mercies are over all his works" (Ps. 145:9).

Jesus is saying the same thing to you today that He said to Bartimaeus: "What can I do for you?" I love that question. It is so simple. He is asking all who would look to Him in faith, "What do you want Me to do for you?"

Jesus is alive and well today, and He is the same yesterday, today, and forever. He is just as anointed and compassionate today as He was when Bartimaeus sat by the roadside begging. The Resurrected Lord, the Messiah, is saying to you, "Receive your healing today! Receive your deliverance today!"

Don't Drop the Ball

I want to warn you of a particular thing that can hinder your ability to receive. You can be reaching out by faith for that Super Bowl pass of God's goodness. You can be well on your way to spiritual victory, but this devilish habit will cause you to fumble and drop the ball.

Jesus warned us about it in Matthew 6:34 NIV when He promised to give us, as kingdom-seekers, everything we need. He said, "Therefore do not worry about tomorrow."

---

15. *"And he could there do no mighty work, save that he laid his hands upon a few sick folk, and healed them. And he marveled because of their unbelief. And he went round about the villages, teaching"* (Mark 6:5, 6). Nazareth would be an exception. We can learn a lesson from this incident. Jesus could do no mighty work there because of their unbelief. He could only heal a few of them. The others were not willing to receive. Was it God's will for them to be sick? No, it was their will. They would not receive Jesus who was sent by the Father to heal them. They refused to believe in Him. What was the solution for unbelief? He began to teach.

Philippians 4:6 NKJV repeats that instruction: "Be anxious for nothing, but in everything by prayer and supplication, with thanksgiving, let your requests be made known to God." First Peter 5:7 adds, "Casting all your care upon him [God]; for he careth for you."

One reason these instructions are so important is because you cannot worry and be in faith at the same time. Worry is a manifestation of fear, and fear contaminates your faith. It is, by definition, doubting that God is going to come through for you.

Obviously, faith and doubt cannot dwell together in the same heart. One of them will have to go. Your heart is your responsibility—you choose.

"But, Gloria," you may say, "you just don't understand how bad my situation is." That may be, but Jesus said you cannot add one measure to your stature, or improve your situation one bit, by worrying about it. On the contrary, it will actually get worse if you keep worrying about it instead of believing God.

Andrew Murray, a wonderful author and man of God, wrote years ago, "I am going to do the will of God every day without thinking of tomorrow." I think that is a wonderful way to live. The truth is, if we will do the will of God today, tomorrow will turn out just great. And the Bible tells us that part of God's will is for us to stop worrying.

When I get under pressure, I make it a point to remember that. Before faith came I used to worry constantly, but I refuse to worry anymore. Why should I worry when God is good and I am endeavoring wholeheartedly to hear and obey Him? He is full of compassion. He is my source! I don't have anything to worry about because He has promised to take care of me.

It would actually be hard for me to worry now. I broke the habit a long time ago. I learned to treat worry as an alcoholic would each time the devil tried to get him to drink again. I would say, "No, I'm not going to do that. I'm not going to indulge in those worried thoughts. I resist them in Jesus' Name." Then I would purposely, by an act of my will, replace those worries with promises from the Word of God.

When I first started learning to be free from worry, I was having a worried thought every few minutes because I had a lot to worry about. We were broke and in debt. We had no future, no hope—nothing. We were born again and I had a Bible, and that was about the extent of our assets. But I saw in that Bible not to worry so I asked God to help me, and when worry came, I would cast it out. I kept doing that even if I had to do it 100 times a day.

You can do the same thing. When thoughts of worry or fear come, don't give them any place. You don't have to receive those negative, unbelieving thoughts the devil brings you. Reject them. Get your Bible and look up the scriptures you are believing. Carry them with you so when you're bombarded with doubt or bad news, you have the Word right there to help you.

You might think that is hard, but if Jairus could do it, you can do it. He did not even have a covenant with God as good as yours! Remember what Jesus said to him when the messengers came to tell him his daughter was dead? He said, "Be not be afraid, only believe" (Mark 5:36).

Under the greatest kind of emotional pressure, Jairus refused worry. He refused fear. He stuck with Jesus and held to his confession of faith.

As a result, he saw the goodness of the Lord invade his life in a miraculous way. There was a resurrection in that situation just like there can be in your situation if you will refuse to fear and believe only.

CHAPTER 9

The New Song

O sing unto the Lord a new song: sing unto the Lord,
all the earth. Sing unto the Lord, bless his name; show forth
his salvation from day to day. Declare his glory among the
heathen, his wonders among all people. For the Lord is
great, and greatly to be praised.

PSALM 96:1–4

As you recall, when we studied examples in the Bible of people who successfully received the goodness of God, we discovered they had three common characteristics. First, we found that each one had received and believed a word from God. Second, each of them acted in a way that revealed their faith in that Word. Third, each successful receiver spoke words of faith. They opened their mouths and said something positive, agreeing with the goodness of the Lord and what they expected to receive from Him.

No doubt, since you are still reading this book, you want to follow their example. You have made up your mind about the goodness of God. You are ready to believe it and you are eager to receive it. If you are like me, you want to receive as much of it as you can as quickly as possible.

I want to close by giving you a spiritual key that will help you do just that. It is a simple but powerful activity that combines all three characteristics of the good receiver. Practice it and it will accelerate your spiritual development. It will increase your capacity to receive from God. It will open the way for His blessing to flood your life more fully and more quickly. It will also make you happier than you have ever been before.

What is this wonderful thing you can do that will so enhance your life?

You can sing a new song. You can open your mouth every day and sing about the goodness of the Lord. You can sing about the blessings He has given you. You can sing out praises and thanksgiving. Sing out your love for Him. You can, simply by singing, open the door ever wider for His glory to fill your life.

Somebody might say, "Oh, now Gloria, get serious. Singing is silly and childish. How powerful can it be as a spiritual tool?"

Powerful enough for the book of Psalms alone to mention it more than seventy times! According to Psalms, singing spiritual songs is not silly at all. On the contrary, the Bible informs us that it is fitting or appropriate for those of us who have been made righteous by the blood of Jesus to sing songs of praise to God. It is the right thing for us to do because He deserves our praise!

Psalm 33:1–5 NIV says:

Sing joyfully to the Lord, you righteous; it is fitting for the upright to praise him. Praise the Lord with the harp; make music to him on the ten-stringed lyre. Sing to him a new song; play skillfully, and shout for joy. For the word of the Lord is right and true; he is faithful in all he does. The

Lord loves righteousness and justice; the earth is full of his unfailing love.

If you have just recently made Jesus your Lord and you are new to the things of God, you may not think you have much to sing about yet. You may not have been in God's kingdom long enough to see much change in your circumstances. You might be thinking, *Hey, I have so many problems, I don't know what to do.*

If that is the case, then sing your way through them!

Even if you were just born again five minutes ago, you have reason to sing, rejoice, and thank the Lord. After all, you are not on the road to hell anymore. You are on the road to heaven! You have a covenant with Almighty God and He has promised to bless you, heal you, prosper you, and deliver you! You know God will keep His promises, so now you have something in life on which you can depend. Where you once were hopeless, now you have a sure hope in Him! You do have something to sing about.

Now that you are a child of God, you can understand revelation from the Word of God. You can put His truth in your heart, let it come out your mouth, and it will change your circumstances. You can be happy in the assurance that once you have God's goodness on the inside of you, things on the outside will have to follow. Problems or not, you are in a great place! So speed up the process by singing to the One who delivers you from all your fears and evil circumstances.

Have a Party in the Presence of the Lord!

One of my favorite verses about singing is found in Psalm 40:1–3:

> I waited patiently for the Lord; and he inclined unto me, and heard my cry. He brought me up also out of an horrible pit, out of the miry clay, and set my feet upon a rock, and established my goings. And he hath put a new song in my mouth, even praise unto our God: many shall see it, and fear, and shall trust in the Lord.

Notice the last verse says that God Himself has put a new song in your mouth. I can tell you from experience, that's the truth. If you will just open your mouth by faith and start singing God's praises, you'll find words coming up out of your heart. Just sing the truth about God. Sing about how wonderful and good He is. Sing His Word back to Him. The more you sing, the more His words will flow, and you will realize you had a new song inside all along. Your song will build you up and strengthen you.

I know that because I've done it. I sing…and sing…and sing to the Lord.

Somebody might say, "I've listened to your preaching tapes and I've never heard you sing."

That's because I don't sing to people; I sing to the Lord. Musically, I'm not especially gifted, but God has the capacity to hear and appreciate my song. It's my love song to Him. When I'm around others, I *speak* my new song. I say words of thanksgiving and praise about Him.

You ought to do the same thing. Whether you choose to sing it or just to speak it, everybody around you ought to hear your new song. If you are born again, you should always have a song of salvation, a song of thanksgiving, a song of deliverance, a song of healing, and a song of prosperity. You should be continually saying things like:

God is so good. He is faithful to me every day. He leads me on in victory and hears me when I pray. He blesses me when I come in and again when I go out. He takes away my old, sad song and gives me a happy shout!

The new song comes out of your heart.

The Bible says when the people of God start singing and talking like that, many people hear and put their trust in Him.

When the world sees a Christian, they ought to see somebody rejoicing. They ought to see somebody who is happy. They ought not to see somebody who looks down and depressed like last year's Christmas tree! Christians are supposed to be glad. We have something to be happy about. We should be dancing and rejoicing.

Not only does our new song open the door for God to bless us, not only does it bless other people—it blesses God, too! He likes it when His people are happy and rejoicing before Him. God likes the rejoicing of His people so much, in fact, that during Old Testament feasts He commanded the Israelites to come into His presence and have a party. It's true! He told them to bring the tithe of their meat and other foods and eat it in His presence. They were to enjoy their blessings and rejoice before Him. Even now, if you go to Israel during feast times, you will find people celebrating. They will be eating good food, singing, dancing, and rejoicing. That is God's idea of a good time!

The Old Testament prophet Joel captured the spirit of God's kind of celebration when he prophesied about the time of Israel's restoration:

> Be glad then, ye children of Zion, and rejoice in the Lord your God: for he hath given you the former rain moderately, and he will cause to come down for you the rain, the former rain, and the latter rain in the first month. And the floors shall be full of wheat, and the vats shall overflow with wine and oil. And I will restore to you the years that the locust hath eaten, the cankerworm, and the caterpillar, and the palmerworm, my great army which I sent among you. And ye shall eat in plenty, and be satisfied, and praise the name of the Lord your God, that hath dealt wondrously with you....
>
> Joel 2:23–26

No Grumbling, Please

Some people miss the blessing the new song brings because they get born again and just keep singing the same old song. They keep saying, "Poor me. Nothing good ever happens to me. I'm broke. I'm sick. I don't know why I don't have a new car. I don't know why I don't have a better house. I don't know why God doesn't take care of me."

That's pitiful! Don't sing that kind of song anymore. That's the old song. It's out-of-date. Put a new song about the goodness of God in your mouth!

If things have been tough for you lately, you might not feel much like singing right now. That's okay. Sing anyway! You'll be surprised how singing a new song will lift your heart. If you'll put the praise of God on your lips, depression will leave you. Doubt will flee and your joy will rise up where it ought to be. The joy of the Lord is your strength! That's what the prophet Ezra declared to the people of Israel in Nehemiah 8:10 AMP: "Then [Ezra] told them, Go your way, eat the fat, drink the sweet drink, and send portions to him for whom nothing is prepared: for this day is holy to our Lord. And be not grieved and depressed, *for the joy of the Lord is your strength and stronghold.*"

Determine that from now on, you'll have the goodness of God in your mouth. Make up your mind that you are not ever going to grumble and complain to God again. Instead, voice praise and thanksgiving.

After all, God is never the problem. He is always good. He is always on time. He never misses it. He is always right. So we ought to be magnifying Him all the time. We ought to be obeying Psalm 35:27: "Let them shout for joy, and be glad, that favour my righteous cause: yea, let them say continually, Let the Lord be magnified, which hath pleasure in the prosperity of his servant."

Do you know what it means to magnify the Lord? It means to focus your heart, mind, and mouth on Him until He is the biggest thing in your life. It means to make Him big in your own sight. You can do that by talking about how great and good He is. Speak the truth about God.

The fact is, no matter how much you magnify God, you will never be able to make Him as big as He really is. You will never be able to overestimate His goodness. God is so big, we will spend eternity exploring Him. He's so great, He exceeds our greatest expectations. He's so good that no matter how good we think He is, we will continually discover He's better than we thought!

Some time ago, Ken and I received a letter from a lady in a former Soviet Union nation who had been watching our television broadcasts. Her letter blessed me tremendously because as I read it, I could practically hear her new song. She overflowed with words of gratitude and praise to God. Even though she was not what most people would consider prosperous, she had become more prosperous. She was thankful for what God had done for her and she believed He could do anything she needed Him to do in her life.

Although I cannot quote the letter exactly, I remember she told us how God had put food on her table and given her a place to live. She wrote about how greatly her life had improved since she had found out about God's goodness and made Jesus her Lord.

Then she said something that really tickled me. Apparently, on one of the television broadcasts she watched, one of the ministers said something about God being able to give you an airplane. (To those of us who are called to preach all over the world, an airplane is a great help!)

In response to that broadcast, she wrote something like this. "I like everything you say and agree with it. But I don't know what I would do with an airplane. It would be so much trouble for me. I'd have to hire a pilot and find a hangar where I could keep the plane. Where would I get gas? Where would I go? It would be difficult to imagine the burden this would be." She just wasn't interested in the hassle.

Isn't that wonderful? It never even occurred to this faith-filled believer that God might not be able to give her an airplane. She knew how big He is. She had magnified Him greatly in her heart and her life. She appreciated Him for what He had already done and she put no limits on what He could do in the future. She didn't doubt He could do it. An airplane just seemed like more trouble than it was worth!

Be Grateful Every Step of the Way

You will never develop that kind of attitude by grumbling and complaining about what God has not done for you yet. You will develop it by actively appreciating the blessings He *has* given you. You will develop it by noticing every little improvement in your life and thanking God for it.

Years ago, when Ken and I were preaching in Nigeria, we were told the Nigerians did not have a word for prosperity. So, when we said *prosperity,* our interpreter would translate it by saying the phrase *to do better.* I like that because, truly, that is what happens when God begins to prosper us. We begin to do better.

That is what happened to Ken and me. When we began serving God, we started where we were and we began to do better. Looking back now, I can see that even after we started doing better, we still had a long way to go because we started out so far behind. But we just stayed in there with God, being grateful, singing our new song. Over the years our circumstances kept improving until now we can say by almost anyone's standards we are doing really well! And we are always increasing.

Am I saying we never murmured or complained? Certainly not. We still get under pressure and have to walk by faith and not by sight. When we speak wrong words, we are quick to repent. When you realize that you are speaking unbelief (words that disagree with God's Word) say, "I break the power of the words I have just spoken, in Jesus' Name. I render them powerless to come to pass. Father, forgive me in the Name of Jesus and cleanse me of all unrighteousness." I am determined that as I continue to believe God to walk in the fullness of His blessing, I will do it with praise in my heart and a song in my mouth.

As children of God, we are never stagnant. No matter how blessed we are, God's promise of increase still stands. We are always increasing if we live in progressive revelation. Greater insight into God's Word brings greater faith, which produces greater blessing. We ask God for a house...and we receive a house. We live in it awhile, then we desire a better house. There's nothing wrong with that. So we ask God for an upgrade. Increase is God's idea.

What is wrong is failing to appreciate what we already have. What is wrong is to give up or to start grumbling because God has not yet given us the fullness of our dream. It is wrong when we start complaining and talking like God is getting slack on the job. That is what got the Israelites in trouble during their wilderness journey: "And ye murmured in your tents, and said, Because the Lord hated us, he hath brought us forth out of the land of Egypt, to deliver us into the hand of the Amorites, to destroy us" (Deut. 1:27). Murmuring does not move God to bless. Murmuring is unbelief.

Rufus Moseley said, "Unbelief is a terrible sin, but it is so prevalent that people don't recognize it as such."[16]

What's more, the New Testament clearly warns us about the dangers of complaining. It says, "We should not tempt the Lord

---

16. Rufus Moseley, *Perfect Everything,* Revised edition (MacAlester Park Pub. Co., 1983).

[try His patience, become a trial to Him, critically appraise Him, and exploit His goodness] as some of them did—and were killed by poisonous serpents; nor discontentedly complain as some of them did—and were put out of the way entirely by the destroyer (death). Now these things befell them by way of a figure [as an example and warning to us]; they were written to admonish and fit us for right action by good instruction, we in whose days the ages have reached their climax (their consummation and concluding period)" (1 Cor. 10:9–11 AMP).

Those verses alone ought to cure us from grumbling forever. They should make us resolve not even to complain in bed at night when we think no one is listening but our husband or wife. We should be loyal to God even when people are not around. After all, God is there. He will hear our complaints, and He will not appreciate them. Our words of unbelief will stop His blessing from working in our lives.

"Well then," you might ask, "what *should* I say when I'm waiting for the Lord to bless me with something—like a new car, for instance—and I haven't received it yet?"

Speak heartfelt words of faith and thanksgiving. Say things like, "Thank You, Lord, for my new car. I believe I've received it and I rejoice over it. Thank You, too, for the car I have now, Father. It's a blessing to me and I appreciate it!"

Fill your mouth with thanksgiving. Jesus said in Mark 11:24 to believe you receive when you pray. What do you do when you receive something? You say, "Thank you!" The appropriate and powerful thing you do after you pray is to be thankful. Maintain a thankful attitude all the time, and it will go a long way in undergirding faith and patience.

Be thankful for what you have already received and are presently enjoying. Be thankful for what you believe you have received that is not yet manifest. See yourself with it. Let it become a reality to you.

I don't know about you, but I enjoy the handiwork of God. When I see a beautiful moon or sunset, it's natural to me to voice my thankfulness. God made the earth for His family to enjoy. I thank Him for the trees as I am enjoying their beauty. And, oh, the flowers are such a blessing to me! "Thank You, Lord."

"Thank You, Lord, for a well body. Thank You for renewing my youth. Thank You that my family is intact, serving You and enjoying Your abundant goodness."

"You are my source, Lord, and I expect miracles today. Thank You for miracles! Thank You for all the good that You continually do for me."

You get the picture. Here are some scriptures to inspire you to thanksgiving:

Colossians 3:15—And let the peace of God rule in your hearts, to the which also ye are called in one body; and be ye thankful.

Romans 1:21—Because that, when they knew God, they glorified him not as God, neither were thankful; but became vain in their imaginations, and their foolish heart was darkened.

Psalm 69:30, 31—I will praise the name of God with a song, and will magnify him with thanksgiving. This also shall please the Lord....

Psalm 95:2—Let us come before his presence with thanksgiving, and make a joyful noise unto him with psalms.

Psalm 100:4, 5—Enter into his gates with thanksgiving, and into his courts with praise: be thankful unto him, and bless his name. For the Lord is good; his mercy is everlasting; and his truth endureth to all generations.

Psalm 107:19–22—Then they cry unto the Lord in their trouble, and he saveth them out of their distresses. He sent his word, and healed them, and delivered them from their destructions. Oh that men would praise the Lord for his goodness, and for his wonderful works to the children of men! And let them sacrifice the sacrifices of thanksgiving, and declare his works with rejoicing.

Psalm 116:17—I will offer to thee the sacrifice of thanksgiving, and will call upon the name of the Lord.

Psalm 147:7—Sing unto the Lord with thanksgiving; sing praise upon the harp unto our God.

Isaiah 51:3—For the Lord shall comfort Zion: he will comfort all her waste places; and he will make her wilderness like Eden, and her desert like the garden of the Lord; joy and gladness shall be found therein, thanksgiving, and the voice of melody.

Jeremiah 30:19—And out of them shall proceed thanksgiving and the voice of them that make merry: and I will multiply them, and they shall not be few; I will also glorify them, and they shall not be small.

Philippians 4:4, 6—Rejoice in the Lord always [delight, gladden yourselves in Him]; again I say, Rejoice!...Do not fret or have any anxiety about anything, but in every circumstance and in everything, by prayer and petition (definite requests), with thanksgiving, continue to make your wants known to God (*The Amplified Bible*).

Colossians 2:6—As ye have therefore received Christ Jesus the Lord, so walk ye in him: rooted and built up in him, and stablished in the faith, as ye have been taught, abounding therein with thanksgiving.

Colossians 4:2—Continue in prayer, and watch in the same with thanksgiving.

Be watchful to be thankful!

When Life Is Like a Dream

You may think I'm going overboard on this subject of singing a new song. You may be thinking, *Come on, now. Everybody has a right to be depressed sometimes. Everybody occasionally sings the blues.*

Not according to the New Testament. It tells us that as believers we are to "Rejoice in the Lord always. Again I will say, rejoice!" (Phil. 4:4 NKJV).

Andrew Murray says, "Joy is not a luxury or a mere accessory in the Christian life. It is the sign that we are really living in God's wonderful love and that that love satisfies us."[17]

Nehemiah 8:10 AMP says, "Be not grieved and depressed, for the joy of the Lord is your strength and stronghold."

We should be continually rejoicing and thanking God for what He's done for us. We should be singing in the shower, singing in

---

17. Andrew Murray, *The Holiest of All,* Abridgment of re-typeset edition, through special arrangement with Baker Books, Grand Rapids, Michigan, (Fort Worth, Texas: Kenneth Copeland Ministries, 1993).

our cars, singing as we go about our work. We should be singing a new song all the time. Forget that old song of doubt, doom, and depression. Refuse to sing it anymore.

That's the way God wants us to be. He wants us so full of victory that we don't just sing someone else's song, but we can spontaneously sing a song from our own heart. He wants us to be so full of His praises that no one has to lead us, no one has to urge us, but we sing to Him because we can't help ourselves. We can have a song in our heart that comes out of our mouth. Proverbs 17:22 says, "A merry heart doeth good like a medicine: but a broken spirit drieth the bones." Whether we are doing it aloud or quietly in our heart, we should be singing a new song all the time.

You might have to begin just by simply choosing to do it. You might have to say, "Bless the Lord, I'm going to sing a new song whether I feel like it or not." But if you will do it wholeheartedly, before long, you *will* feel like it. You will start remembering how bad things were when you found God. You will start thinking about what He has done for you since then. You will get excited about what He is going to do for you in the days ahead and you will want to sing!

If you will keep singing that song, if you will keep going with God, refusing to be drawn off by disobedience or unbelief, you will find yourself walking in your dreams. You will look around and see the goodness of God poured out in every area of your life. You will see His goodness everywhere you turn. You will be living out His plan, enjoying His provision and dwelling in the place He prepared especially for you.

You will be living proof to the world that "happy is that people, whose God is the Lord" (Ps. 144:15). Your neighbors will see the joy and blessing that marks your life. They will hear you singing your new song morning, noon, and night, and they will be drawn to the Lord. Psalm 126:1–2 says it this way:

> When the Lord turned again the captivity of Zion, we were like them that dream. Then was our mouth filled with laughter, and our tongue with singing: then said they among the heathen, The Lord hath done great things for them.

That is the way God always intended it to be. From the beginning, it has been His will to have a people He could bless so lavishly that their very lives would be a testimony to the world of His goodness.

If we as believers today will put ourselves in position to receive, we can be the people God has longed to have. We can be those who dare to believe and receive His abundant blessings. We can be those who cause the heathen to say, "Surely, God is a good God!"

Psalm 115:10–16 says:

> O house of Aaron, trust in the Lord: he is their help and their shield. Ye that fear the Lord, trust in the Lord: he is their help and their shield. The Lord hath been mindful of us: he will bless us; he will bless the house of Israel; he will bless the house of Aaron. He will bless them that fear the Lord, both small and great. The Lord shall increase you more and more, you and your children. Ye are blessed of the Lord which made heaven and earth. The heaven, even the heavens, are the Lord's: but the earth hath he given to the children of men.

God has you on His mind. He is thinking about your increase and the good He would enjoy bringing into your life. Become that receiver we talked about earlier. Stretch out your hands toward heaven, the place from which comes your help. Put yourself in position to receive all that God desires to do in your life. You will be able to say with David, the man after God's own heart:

I will extol thee, my God, O king; and I will bless thy name for ever and ever. Every day will I bless thee; and I will praise thy name for ever and ever. Great is the Lord, and greatly to be praised; and his greatness is unsearchable. One generation shall praise thy works to another, and shall declare thy mighty acts. I will speak of the glorious honour of thy majesty, and of thy wondrous works. And men shall speak of the might of thy terrible acts: and I will declare thy greatness. They shall abundantly utter the memory of thy great goodness, and shall sing of thy righteousness. The Lord is gracious, and full of compassion; slow to anger, and of great mercy. The Lord is good to all: and his tender mercies are over all his works. All thy works shall praise thee, O Lord; and thy saints shall bless thee. They shall speak of the glory of thy kingdom, and talk of thy power; to make known to the sons of men his mighty acts, and the glorious majesty of his kingdom. Thy kingdom is an everlasting kingdom, and thy dominion endureth throughout all generations. The Lord upholdeth all that fall, and raiseth up all those that be bowed down. The eyes of all wait upon thee; and thou givest them their meat in due season. Thou openest thine hand, and satisfiest the desire of every living thing. The Lord is righteous in all his ways, and holy in all his works. The Lord is nigh unto all them that call upon him, to all that call upon him in truth. He will fulfil the desire of them that fear him: he also will hear their cry, and will save them. The Lord preserveth all them that love him: but all the wicked will he destroy. My mouth shall speak the praise of the Lord: and let all flesh bless his holy name for ever and ever.

Psalm 145:1–21

God is good to all. That means you!

Prayer for Salvation and Baptism in the Holy Spirit

Heavenly Father, I come to You in the Name of Jesus. Your Word says, "Whosoever shall call on the name of the Lord shall be saved" (Acts 2:21). I am calling on You. Jesus, come into my heart and be Lord over my life according to Romans 10:9–10. "If thou shalt confess with thy mouth the Lord Jesus, and shalt believe in thine heart that God hath raised him from the dead, thou shalt be saved. For with the heart man believeth unto righteousness; and with the mouth confession is made unto salvation." I do that now. I confess that Jesus is Lord, and I believe in my heart that God raised Him from the dead.

I am now reborn! I am a Christian—a child of Almighty God! I am saved! You also said in Your Word, "If ye then, being evil, know how to give good gifts unto your children: HOW MUCH MORE shall your heavenly Father give the Holy Spirit to them that ask him?" (Luke 11:13). I'm also asking You to fill me with the Holy Spirit. Holy Spirit, rise up within me as I praise God. I fully expect to speak with other tongues as You give me the utterance (Acts 2:4). In Jesus' Name. Amen!

Begin to praise God for filling you with the Holy Spirit. Speak those words and syllables you receive—not in your own language, but the language given to you by the Holy Spirit. You have to use your own voice. God will not force you to speak. Don't be concerned with how it sounds. It is a heavenly language!

Continue with the blessing God has given you and pray in the spirit every day.

You are a born-again, Spirit-filled believer. You'll never be the same!

Find a good church that boldly preaches God's Word and obeys it. Become a part of a church family who will love and care for you as you love and care for them.

We need to be connected to each other. It increases our strength in God. It's God's plan for us.

Make it a habit to watch the *Believer's Voice of Victory* television broadcast and become a doer of the Word who is blessed in his doing (James 1:22–25).

Questions for Reflection and Discussion

CHAPTER 1: UNDERSTANDING GOD'S GOODNESS—THE FOUNDATION OF FAITH

1. Why is it important for you to understand the depth of God's goodness? How will this knowledge change you?
2. Are you afraid to trust God wholly with your life's circumstances? If so, why?
3. Have you believed God is the source of all things, good and bad, that happen to us? Do you see now what that belief says about God? Is it true?
4. How does Psalm 23 give you courage? What does it help you face today?
5. For what situation can you begin to believe in the goodness of the Lord today?

CHAPTER 2: WILL THE REAL GOD PLEASE STAND UP?

1. Have you believed that God is angry with you? How do you feel to discover that He is only good and wants only good for you?
2. Why is God jealous for those who love Him? What is the result when God's people try to love other gods as well?

3. Why does God want you to worship and obey Him? Is it to keep you in line?

4. How does it feel to know that "God's hopes are fadeless where we are concerned"?

5. Have you ever regretted choosing to obey God?

CHAPTER 3: TRACKING GOD'S GOODNESS THROUGH THE BIBLE

1. What does the Creation account tell us about what God wants to give His family?

2. Even when mankind sinned, did God desire good or evil for His people? How do you know this?

3. What did the Ten Commandments and Levitical law provide for God's people?

4. Has God changed through the many years since Adam and Eve? Do you believe He is still all good, and wants all good for you? What is the evidence of that?

5. What can you determine about God's goodness by looking at the numerous opportunities He gave Israel to repent?

CHAPTER 4: BLESSINGS STORED UP FOR YOU

1. In what ways do humans limit the expression of God's goodness on earth?

2. How do you feel about the "ocean of goodness" God wants to pour out on you?

3. What role does the Holy Spirit play in helping you understand God's immense goodness?

4. Why does God want people to see and hear about His goodness in His people's lives?

5. How will the knowledge that "people are hungry for joy" change the way you live?

CHAPTER 5: A GOOD PLAN AND A GOOD PLACE

1. Were you surprised to learn that God cares about the home you occupy? Why?

2. How do you feel about the fact that God "wants you to walk in your dreams"? What are your dreams? Have you prayed about them?

3. What "equipment" has God built into you to use in His ministry?

4. Why is it you cannot progress far in your spiritual life without the Holy Spirit?

5. From Israel's history, what can you learn about God as a planner?

CHAPTER 6: ENJOYING GOD'S BEST

1. How have you seen Satan attacking your life of faith? What helps you withstand his attacks?

2. Do you find yourself operating in life more by faith, or by fear? What are the consequences?

3. Have you ever said, "The devil made me do it"? Why is that statement never true?

4. Have you ever stepped outside the "circle of blessing"? What happened?

5. What does this statement mean: "God is never the problem"?

CHAPTER 7: THE KEY TO HEAVEN'S STOREHOUSE

1. How were you affected by the account of Grandma Martha's life? Is there a habit of hers you would like to adopt?
2. Do you live in total dependence upon God, or do you trust in yourself or others to supply all your needs?
3. Describe what it means to seek first the kingdom of God. How can you make this a lifestyle?
4. Do you tend to learn about the Lord by listening to someone else's experiences or do you learn about Him by fellowshiping *with Him*? Why is it important to learn both ways?
5. What gives you the ability to lead a godly life—is it only your willpower or something else even stronger?

CHAPTER 8: LOOKING FOR A RECEIVER

1. Have you ever thought that "God has in His hand blessings beyond human comprehension. He is longing to pass them to His family"? Are you a willing receiver of God's blessings?
2. What does it mean to "assimilate [the Scriptures] through your mind and senses"? How will doing this help you?
3. What will happen to Satan if you let the Word of God into your eyes, ears, and heart?
4. What part does patience play in making you a good receiver?
5. What do you need from God today? How can you put yourself in a position to receive it from Him?

CHAPTER 9: THE NEW SONG

1. What three things must you do to successfully receive blessings from God?

2. If you are in a difficult circumstance, what can you sing about to hasten the blessing of the Lord?

3. When we sing the Lord's praises, who is blessed besides ourselves?

4. What does it mean to "magnify the Lord"?

5. Is joy an option or a necessity? Why?

About the Author

Gloria Copeland is a noted author and minister of the gospel whose teaching ministry is known throughout the world. Believers worldwide know her through Believers' Conventions, Victory Campaigns, magazine articles, teaching audios and videos, and the daily and Sunday *Believer's Voice of Victory* television broadcast, which she hosts with her husband, Kenneth Copeland. She is known for "Healing School," which she began teaching and hosting in 1979 at KCM meetings. Gloria delivers the Word of God and the keys to victorious Christian living to millions of people every year.

Gloria has written many books, including *God's Will for You, Walk With God, God's Will Is Prosperity, Hidden Treasures, Living Contact,* and *Are You Listening?* She has also co-authored several books with her husband, including *Family Promises, Healing Promises,* and the best-selling daily devotionals, *From Faith to Faith* and *Pursuit of His Presence.*

She holds honorary doctorates from Oral Roberts University, Miami Bible Institute, and Life Christian University. In 1994, Gloria was voted Christian Woman of the Year, an honor conferred on women whose example demonstrates outstanding Christian leadership. Gloria is also the co-founder and vice president of Kenneth Copeland Ministries in Fort Worth, Texas.

Learn more about
Kenneth Copeland Ministries
by visiting our Web site
at **www.kcm.org.**

World Offices of
Kenneth Copeland Ministries

For more information about KCM and a free catalog, please write
the office nearest you:

Kenneth Copeland Ministries
Fort Worth, Texas 76192-0001

Kenneth Copeland
Locked Bag 2600
Mansfield Delivery Centre
QUEENSLAND 4122
AUSTRALIA

Kenneth Copeland
Private Bag X 909
FONTAINEBLEAU
2032
REPUBLIC OF
SOUTH AFRICA

Kenneth Copeland
Post Office Box 3111
STN LCD #1
Langley, B.C. V3A 4R3
CANADA

Kenneth Copeland Ministries
Post Office Box 84
L'VIV 79000
UKRAINE

Kenneth Copeland
Post Office Box 15
BATH
BA1 3XN
U.K.

We're Here for You!

Believer's Voice of Victory
Television Broadcast

Join Kenneth and Gloria Copeland and the *Believer's Voice of Victory* broadcasts Monday through Friday and on Sunday each week, and learn how faith in God's Word can take your life from ordinary to extraordinary. This teaching from God's Word is designed to get you where you want to be—on top!

You can catch the "Believer's Voice of Victory" broadcast on your local, cable, or satellite channels.

Check your local listings for times and stations in your area.

Believer's Voice of Victory Magazine

Enjoy inspired teaching and encouragement from Kenneth and Gloria Copeland and guest ministers each month in the *Believer's Voice of Victory* magazine. Also included are real-life testimonies of God's miraculous power and divine intervention in the lives of people just like you!

It's more than just a magazine—it's a ministry.

To receive a Free subscription to
Believer's Voice of Victory, write to:

Kenneth Copeland Ministries
Fort Worth, Texas 76192-0001

Or call: 1-800-600-7395 (7 a.m.-5 p.m. CT)
Or visit our Web site at www.kcm.org.

If you are writing from outside the U.S., please contact the KCM office nearest you. Addresses for all Kenneth Copeland Ministries offices are listed on the previous pages.